FEARLESS

FEARLESS

One Woman,
One Kayak,
One Continent

JOE GLICKMAN

FALCONGUIDES ®

GUILFORD, CONNECTICUT
HELENA, MONTANA
AN IMPRINT OF GLOBE PEQUOT PRESS

FALCONGUIDES®

Copyright © 2012 by Joe Glickman

Falcon Guides is an imprint of Globe Pequot Press.
Falcon, FalconGuides, and Outfit Your Mind are registered trademarks of Morris Book Publishing, LLC

Layout artist: Justin Marciano
Project editors: Gregory Hyman & Meredith Dias

Maps by Melissa Baker © Morris Book Publishing, LLC

Library of Congress Cataloging-in-Publication Data

Glickman, Joe.
  Fearless : one woman, one kayak, one continent / Joe Glickman.
    p. cm.
  ISBN 978-0-7627-7287-2
  1. Hoffmeister, Freya, 1964- 2. Women athletes—Biography. 3. Sea kayakers—Biography. 4. Sea kayaking—Australia. 5. Voyages and travels—Australia. I. Title.
  GV697.H64G55 2012
  797.1224092—dc23
  [B]
                                          2011035891

Printed in the United States of America

10 9 8 7 6 5 4 3 2 1

He is able who thinks he is able.

—Buddha

Always back the horse named self-interest, son. It'll be the only one trying.

—J. T. Lang, two-time premier of New South Wales

TABLE OF CONTENTS

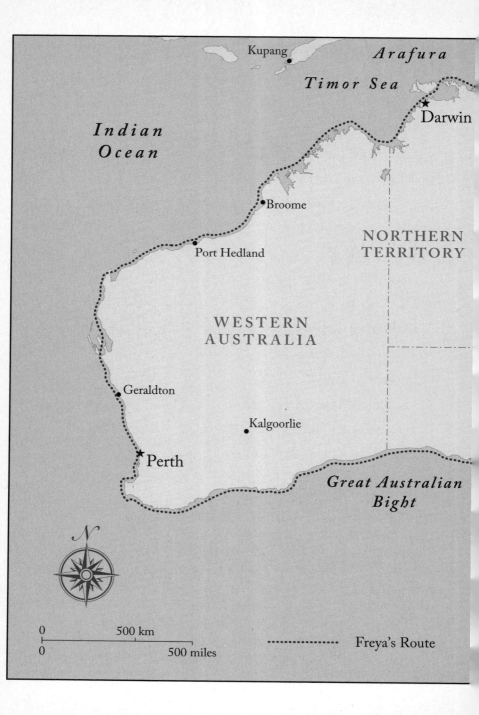

Kupang

Arafura

Timor Sea

★ Darwin

*Indian
Ocean*

• Broome

• Port Hedland

NORTHERN
TERRITORY

WESTERN
AUSTRALIA

• Geraldton

Kalgoorlie •

★ Perth

*Great Australian
Bight*

N

| 0 | 500 km |
| 0 | 500 miles |

••••••••• Freya's Route

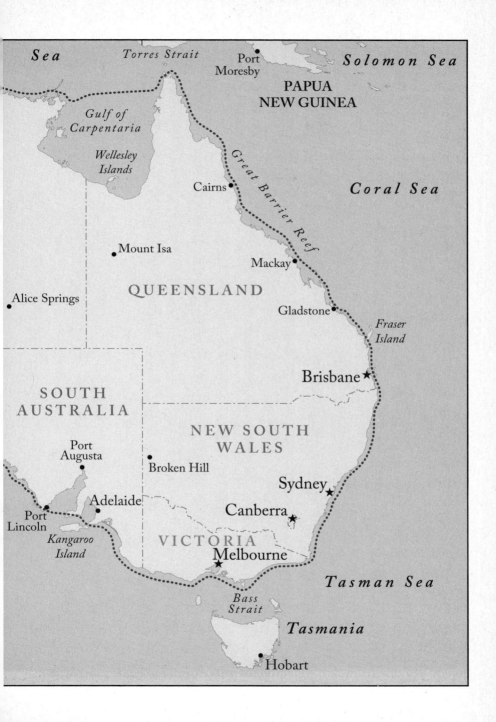

CHAPTER 1

The Freya Factor

Only dead fish swim with the stream.

—GERMAN PROVERB

BY THE TIME FREYA HOFFMEISTER WAS SIX YEARS OLD, SHE COULD WALK on her hands around her family's neat, two-bedroom home in Heikendorf, Germany. When she turned sixteen and had grown too large to continue competing as a gymnast, she earned her hunting license and became something of a local Annie Oakley, a deadeye for clay pigeons. She sped around Germany on a motorcycle in a tight red leather suit, finished sixth in the Miss Germany pageant, and competed as a bodybuilder. When she was twenty-three she began skydiving, and she eventually married her instructor. Ten years and fifteen hundred jumps later, including the first-ever tandem jump over the North Pole, she hung up her harness when she learned she was pregnant.

Kayaking would become her next obsession. She learned to paddle with her son in the back hatch, toiling in the Baltic Sea off the coast of her hometown and in nearby rivers. She discovered Greenland-style rolling and mastered all thirty-two rolls in two years—half the time it takes most people. She even invented a few moves, like balancing her paddle on her head while standing in the boat and, better yet, performing a headstand in the cockpit. In 2006 she flew to the Greenland Kayaking Championship in Sisimuit, Greenland, entered eight competitions, and won eight gold medals.

The following year she flew to Iceland with a boyfriend, a paddling instructor from Florida named Greg Stamer. They began their trip with a

55-mile crossing of Faxaflói Bay—a first by kayak. The next day, they set out across Breidafjordur Bay. With 16 miles to go, a frigid 20-mph headwind slowed them to a crawl, and they wound up spending twenty-two hours on the water. Paddling with dolphins and whales, alongside waterfalls, cliffs, and icebergs, they notched the fastest circumnavigation of Iceland, covering 1,007 miles in thirty-three days. Stamer was impressed by the landscape and scope of the challenge. Freya dubbed the journey "easy" and "more or less boring."

Throughout, they squabbled like an old married couple. "Freya and I are both competitive," said Stamer, "and it wasn't long before each day became a stage race." As they racked up the miles, they began acting more like competitors and less like a team. Not surprisingly, the relationship did not survive the trip.

Freya decided her next trip would be solo so she could do things her way, no argument needed. She settled on a circumnavigation of New Zealand's South Island, a *Lord of the Rings* landscape of rain forest, snow-capped mountains, glacial valleys, and frigid rivers. The sea on the west coast is known for its gale force winds and dangerous surf, which may explain why only three solo paddlers, all male, had made it around. Freya wanted to be the first female; halfway around a reporter informed her that she was on pace to break the record held by New Zealand's paddling legend Paul Caffyn.[*] Freya got smashed in the surf, busted her boat, and lost a paddle, but she covered the last 103 miles in thirty-one hours and broke the record by six days. Caffyn, who greeted her at the finish with champagne, called her seventy-day effort "the most significant solo kayak trip undertaken by a woman in the Southern Hemisphere."

But it was only a warm-up. In 2009, at the age of forty-four, Freya Hoffmeister flew to Sydney, loaded her kayak on the roof of a rental car, and drove ten hours to "Caffyn's Cove" in Melbourne, where twenty-seven years earlier her friend began the journey that was the jewel in his paddling crown, a solo circumnavigation so audacious that some refused

---

[*] Caffyn was born in Sydney and grew up near Brisbane but has lived alone for decades by the Tasman Sea on the west coast of New Zealand's South Island.

to believe he had actually done it. It took Caffyn 360 days to complete the 9,420-mile circuit. Freya aimed to do it faster. And without support.

———

I first learned of the Hoffmeister phenomenon in a short article about her South Island trip and went to her website to find out more. I'm a freelance writer and marathon kayak racer and have known for some time that the word *kayak*—*qajaq* to the Inuits who hunted from boats made of seal skin and whale bone twenty-five hundred years before Christ first cussed—is spelled the same backwards and forwards. From my investigation of Freya's website, two facts became clear: She had as many gear sponsors as Madonna has had lovers and was equally bold when it came to displaying her female charms. In one picture she's straddling her black kayak with a suggestive smile; in another, her wrists are lashed to the paddle. In a series of shots taken at a trade show, she's mingling with admirers in a custom-designed black neoprene dress zipped up the front. And in the pièce de résistance, she's posing on tippy toes in front of a boulder in a sleeveless wetsuit, a pair of paddles crossed at her crotch.

I couldn't decide if she was an exhibitionist, an egomaniac, or just a good-looking jock with a ribald sense of humor, but I smelled a story and wrote to see if I could get an interview. In the course of our e-mail exchange I mentioned that I was headed to Puerto Rico to compete in a surf ski race—a 24-mile open ocean race from the island of Culebra to the main island. Freya had never paddled one of these narrow, sit-on-top ocean racing kayaks—she barely knew what they looked like—but she was intrigued and, as I was about to learn, with Freya that's all it takes. She arrived in San Juan eight days before the race and started racking up miles in the ski.

When she stepped out of the elevator in the hotel lobby the night I arrived, I didn't have to look for a name tag. She's 5′10″ and 165 pounds with high cheekbones, blue eyes, and striated shoulders. She reminded me of the East German Olympic swimmers I watched as a kid—large, muscular, powerful—only with shiny red toenails, a Maori necklace made of bone, and a silver kayak pendant. In open-toed platform shoes, she nearly looked me in the eye and I'm 6′4″.

Over the next couple of days, when we weren't training or hanging out with the other paddlers, I gathered information for my story. I'm often in the company of athletic women, but I'd never come across a combination of jock and siren quite like this. Freya didn't exactly flirt with me while we were in Puerto Rico, but she didn't *not* flirt with me either . . . or with four-time Olympic medalist Greg Barton or South African Ian Gray, the eventual race winner, or the other buff men she rubbed elbows with in the days before the race. But you'd have to be a gay guy with a seeing-eye dog to miss the aura of *ooh-la-la* that hovered around her, an aura she created as much with her words as with the form-fitting black tank tops she favored. "I'm a powerful woman who sometimes needs a strong shoulder to lean on," she told me. Fair enough. But she also described herself as "a man-eater," after which she laughed coquettishly. And even when the topic wandered to other subjects, she managed to keep things carnal through the use of her favorite adjective, "sexy":

Rolling a sea kayak was sexy.

Her sleek new surf ski was sexy.

"Dancing blind with waves" during an all-night paddle was "sensual."

Rough water was sexy: "The rougher the better," she said. "I like it *big* out there!"

Double entendres aside, it was clear from our training runs she did like it big. She was paddling an unfamiliar, less stable type of boat in rough conditions in the company of far more experienced paddlers, but I saw not a speck of fear or self-doubt. This was, after all, someone who said that paddling around Iceland was easy and boring, a statement I had a hard time accepting. Every time I head out into rough open water, from the Great Lakes to Tahiti to South Africa, as surely as I'll get wet, I'll be afraid—often very afraid. So as we sat poolside during our first official interview, I challenged her on that point. "Did you find it intimidating to cross Faxaflói Bay? At one point you were 20 miles off shore."

"Not a bit," she replied, without pausing to consider the question.

4

Was she lying or just trying to be provocative? Or could she simply be ignorant? As unlikely as it seemed, maybe she didn't know how dangerous the famed Icelandic winds could be. I told her about my friend Marcus Demuth, who tried paddling around Iceland the year after Freya did. Six days out, when a wave slammed him onto a rocky shore, he lost not only his spare paddle but the pager on which he had been receiving weather forecasts. A few days later he was caught out at sea in a sudden storm, with offshore winds gusting to 60 mph. For three panic-stricken hours he fought through the frigid waves, barely moving forward, landing finally on a treeless island. He was stranded there for four days, buffeted by the wind and spray from breaking waves. When the storm finally passed, he paddled to shore, caught a bus to Reykjavik, and flew home. "Most human beings," I said, "would experience genuine fear in a situation like that."

Freya didn't know Marcus from a penguin with sunglasses, but from this story, she surmised that he was "weak."

"We were lucky," she said, "we had good weather. But I would never quit."

"Near-death experiences tend to shake a guy's confidence," I said.

Freya sipped her pina colada and leaned back, ready to change the subject. "I got a bit tired on the crossing. But . . . what's the problem?" Which, with her accent, sounded like *Vasdaproblum?* It's a phrase she uses all the time, and it means that further probing for emotional nuance will be a waste of time.

"Well, if you'd disappeared at sea it would have looked bad on your resume," I muttered. In my notebook I scribbled: *Blunt, dismissive—and fearless??*

I thought for a second about how different paddling would be if I was truly without fear, and for another second about how different life would be. Then I wrote, *Explore further.*

❦

As a new surf ski paddler Freya was eager to improve, but she ignored all of my advice, including the suggestion to change her all-black paddling attire for gear better suited to the blazing sun. Black may be slimming, but it was well over 90 degrees. And although this would be her first race in a surf ski, and her initial goal was not to finish last, as the race drew near she began talking about beating female favorite Anitza Villalobos, a younger, faster woman who hoped to represent Puerto Rico in the Olympics. I thought this goal was unrealistic. But, doing it her way, she easily managed the 24-mile crossing from Culebra to Puerto del Ray in rough, *oh–so–sexy,* downwind conditions. In fact, she finished just five minutes behind Villalobos, an impressive performance for a sea kayaker in her first surf ski race.

Ten minutes later she had sufficiently recovered from three hours of toiling under the sun to walk on her hands around the pool like a circus seal. After she righted herself, a woman from Deutschland greeted Freya cordially in their native tongue. Freya turned cold. "I'm sorry, I don't speak German on holiday," she said, and walked away, leaving her countrywoman hanging.

I took a mental note. *Doesn't speak German away from home. And isn't nice about it.*

<hr>

At the post-race dinner later that night, I chatted with paddling legend Greg Barton about the next big race on the calendar—a 32-mile open-ocean crossing from the island of Molokai to Oahu. Freya wanted to know more. "It's the unofficial world championship of ocean racing," I explained. "It's the roughest surf ski race out there."

Maybe it was my choice of words, but Freya immediately asked, "What is the date?" and pulled out her smartphone. But it turned out that on the day of the race she was scheduled to be a guest instructor at a sea kayak symposium in Italy.

Lucky you, I thought. Navigating the Molokai channel can take the world's best paddlers four hours. As the South Pacific, after rolling uninterrupted for thousands of miles, funnels between the islands of Oahu and Molokai, the swell routinely reaches heights of 15 to 20 feet. Meanwhile, the trade winds are blowing perpendicular to the swell. If you can use wind-generated runners to accelerate onto one of these swift-rolling giants, you can go screaming (literally) across the ocean at 20 mph—half man, half fly-ing fish. That's the allure of the channel. Of course, if you drop down the face too fast, the boat may pitch pole, ejecting you like a pea from a plastic spoon.

The first time I did the race in 2003, I capsized so often I would have been better off with goggles and swim fins; it was a humbling, humiliating experience. I trained harder and returned the following May and idioti-cally agreed to compete in a warm-up race along the Kauai coast the day after I arrived. I was grinding to the finish, roughly 2 miles out to sea, when a wave sprang up over a reef and dropped on my head with such force my ski snapped nearly in half. Caught in the break zone, I was get-ting darn close to drowning when a buddy came to my aid. To add insult to coral rash, it cost $750 to repair the boat I had borrowed.

What I'm getting at is Molokai is not a race for a beginning ski paddler.

But Freya started rearranging her schedule. She made a phone call, sent an e-mail, and before you could say *Queen Lydia Kamaka'eha Kaola Mali'I Lili'uokalani* she announced: "I will go!"

Wow. In the time it would take me to decide on my entrée, Freya had decided to take on a serious challenge, one that would require a consider-able investment of time and money. When I described this to Greg Stamer in an e-mail exchange after I got home, he wasn't surprised. "Freya con-sumes life with the intensity and passion of a terminally ill patient who is looking to fill every remaining minute with excitement," is how he put it. At dinner that night, I opened my notebook and wrote, *Doesn't fuck around.*

❧

I had plenty of material for a story—a paddling beauty queen who could walk on her hands, jump out of airplanes, and shoot a squirrel between the eyes with a .22. But then Freya began talking about her next trip, and suddenly I had a new lead.

Long before I met Freya, I read Paul Caffyn's *The Dreamtime Voy-age*, a detailed account (with stunning photos) of his year-long journey around Oz, as Australia is commonly called. The lanky Kiwi endured

---

* After a decade of trying to interest a publisher in his book, Caffyn self-published his book in 1994.

shark attacks, saltwater crocodiles, deadly jellyfish, sea snakes, huge surf, and a tropical cyclone that nearly removed him from the planet. Along the three 100-mile stretches of unbroken cliffs, he popped No-Doz like M&Ms to stay awake. *Paddler* magazine ranked it the third toughest sea kayak trip of all time, behind two solo crossings of the Atlantic in 1928 and 1956. As John Dowd, the author of *Sea Kayaking: A Manual for Long Distance Touring*, said: "Every day he could have quit and he didn't. His trip is in another league."

I'm down with the whole long-distance, man-versus-nature, journey of self-exploration thing. I've cycled across the United States, paddled from Montana to New York, and climbed Mount McKinley in Alaska, and I'm always on the lookout for the next epic trip. But Caffyn's adventure seemed so physically punishing and psychically draining that any fantasy I'd had of becoming the second human to complete the circuit evaporated halfway through the third chapter of his book.

Evidently Caffyn's sober, gritty tome had had the opposite effect on Freya. Before completing her South Island trip, she had started thinking about the North Island. Only Caffyn had rounded both. But during the week she stayed with the bearded, bespectacled bachelor at his home on the Tasman Sea, she began reading *The Dreamtime Voyage*. And with each page she grew more convinced that Australia would be next. She had started talking to potential sponsors, but it wasn't a done deal—yet.

I didn't think she had nearly enough experience. "You're talking a quantum leap in difficulty," I said. "It's like thinking you can climb Everest because you've made it up Mount Rainier."

But in Freya's mind, if it could be done—and Caffyn had shown that it could—there was no reason she couldn't do it. "I made it around the South Island faster than Paul," she said. "Why couldn't I do the same around Oz?"

I could think of many reasons, but I started with the obvious. "It's 8,000 miles longer than the South Island and far more dangerous."

"Very funny," Freya said.

Huh? That's normally one of my favorite compliments, but what had I said to deserve it? I told her about my friend Eric Stiller, the owner of Manhattan Kayak Company in the Big Apple, who had attempted to round

Oz in a double kayak with an Aussie named Tony Brown. In the first two months, he and Brown hit the tail end of a cyclone. They capsized in monstrous surf and mangled their boat. They were covered with saltwater rashes and blisters and Brown developed a painful fungus under his nails. Eric, who began the trip with less body fat than a welterweight, lost 22 pounds. The beleaguered pair made it from Sydney to Darwin—the equivalent of paddling from New York to Los Angeles, but still roughly 6,000 miles short of their goal—before calling it quits. They were lucky to have survived. "It's a dangerous route," I said. "And because you're out there so long, the chances of something going wrong are really high."

If I had not yet realized I was wasting my breath, her reply, "*Vasdaproblum?*" should have tipped me off. But I persevered. I pointed out that before Caffyn tackled Oz he'd paddled around the North and South Islands of New Zealand and Great Britain.* "Stick to your original plan," I said, "paddle the North Island, sharpen your skills and then try Oz."

Her response was to ask me if I'd like to drive her support vehicle for a year.

⌁

Two weeks before Molokai, I asked via e-mail if she was ready for Hawaii. "I haven't paddled at all," she replied, adding a ☺ icon. Preparations for her trip, "Race Around Australia," were in full swing. She was consumed with ordering gear, contacting sponsors, and organizing topo maps and charts for her GPS. "Besides it's too cold, flat, and boring here to train. ☹"

The day before she was to fly out, she wrote: "I'm getting fat! I hope my ass will fit in the seat. Otherwise it will be fine. ☺"

She's dead meat, I thought.

And although it turned out I was right, her problems had nothing to do with paddling. Freya in Waikiki was like Paris Hilton in the bush, only in reverse: She griped about the crowds, the cost of the hotel, eating in restaurants, waiting around to train. Most of us were staying at a

---

* After Australia he circumnavigated the four main islands of Japan, Alaska, Greenland, and New Caledonia.

hotel that gave discounts to paddlers on the outskirts of Waikiki, where the tacky tourist scene was unavoidable, as I had explained during the minuscule gap between Freya's hearing about the race and deciding to go. So what if the other tourists were watching fake hula or piling their plates high at a faux luau? We were training in the world's best aquatic playground with a world-class field of paddlers for the world's most storied ocean race. Freya wasn't inclined to look on the bright side and complained more or less constantly.

But it was worse than that.

When Freya announced she was coming to Hawaii, I feared that she would struggle socially with the fast-talking, wisecracking Aussies and South Africans who dominated the field, and indeed she did. Her English was good, but she was confounded by the Aussies, who seemed to fill their mouths with marbles each morning when they got up. Even I blanked when a bloke said: *G'daymatewhereyafromWagga?* And the guttural *aa haa kaa* of the Afrikaners—the "Dutchmen" from South Africa—could sometimes leave me staring like my dog Sylvie when I ask her if she's a good girl. Even when Freya could follow the words, she couldn't get the jokes.

The clothes didn't help, either. In the (mostly) geeky, male-dominated world of sea kayaking, Freya's Amazon playgirl persona worked wonders. The first time Greg Stamer met her at a rolling clinic, she wore an all-black neoprene suit with a snug hood that framed her striking face and knee-high neoprene boots with white laces. Later in the evening, she accessorized her outfit with a large hunting knife strapped on her hip. "She looked like an action hero," he said. Another admirer blogged: "Freya's lady-or-the-tiger quality has caused many a man to consider forsaking his marriage vows."

Other women in the paddling world have made notable trips, but none have received nearly as much attention. Freya had branded herself "The Woman in Black" on her website, and in Hawaii she stuck with the winning formula. But in the ultimate beach community, amidst a sea of baggy shorts and flip-flops, Freya's black spandex tights, tank tops, and platform shoes made her seem both over- and underdressed. To the buff young male paddlers, she was more an object of curiosity than desire.

But it was worse than that.

She was a sea kayaker who knew nothing about racing. She didn't drink coffee or beer—the elixirs that allowed us to transform killing time into hanging out. She cut to the front of lines, and I once saw her casually wipe her sunglasses on the shirttail of a woman she barely knew. More importantly, she seemed unable or unwilling to carry on a conversation that wasn't about her. In Puerto Rico, it worked because I had been interviewing her essentially all the time. But in Hawaii, her self-absorption was oppressive; she now seemed to assume I would want to continue our one-sided conversation indefinitely. I had created a monster, and the monster had followed me to Hawaii.

The nightmare started my first morning over coffee with Herman Chalupsky. Let me take a moment to introduce the Chalupsky brothers. A 6′4″, 220-pound South African with leading-man good looks, Herman is a two-time Molokai winner and the younger, quieter brother of the eleven-time winner and shameless self-promoter Oscar Chalupsky. I had met the Chalupsky boys in 1996 at a race in northern Quebec. The course was a brutal 36 miles, straight across the frigid St. Lawrence, and for nearly five hours Oscar and Herman hammered away side by side until Herman broke away to claim the $10,000 first prize. Oscar didn't take the loss well and later that night at a bar, when he saw Herman also likely to score with a local *jeune fille*, it was all too much. He huffily announced that he was leaving that minute to drive back to Boston in the car they had rented together, although it was 1:30 a.m. and he'd had at least twelve beers. Herman pondered his options: Drive 600 miles through the night with his brooding brother or carry on with the j.f.? Herman followed Oscar outside, returned with his suitcase, and made his way back to Boston on his own the next day.

A few days later Oscar called, and I asked him how his drive had been.

"World class," he said, as if he had planned it all along. He had traveled through the night, slept a few hours, clocked half a pot of coffee, and played eighteen brilliant holes of golf. Or so he said.

That, in a nutshell, is Oscar: arrogant and full of crap on the one hand, and supremely capable and boundlessly optimistic on the other. Herman had spent enough years in the bombastic shadow of the Big O to have developed a very low tolerance for self-congratulation of any kind. He and Freya were destined to not get along.

Admittedly, talking to Herman is an acquired taste and requires special skills. He's brooding, profane, and acerbic and, don't ask me why, peppers his speech with cockney rhyme. So if you don't know that *one's 'n two's* are "shoes," *gun 'n trigger* is "figure," or *five-to-two* is "Jew," then as far as comprehension goes you're up the creek without a *tube of glue*—or "clue."

When Freya pulled up a chair that first morning, I believe we were in the middle of discussing the pros and cons of breast implants. We paused, with all due respect, and Freya took the opportunity to launch into a somewhat lengthy description of her race in Puerto Rico. I'm not sure if that's what sent Herman into "bugger off" mode, or if it was just his sketchy personality, but conversational rigor mortis descended like fog in Reykjavik. I eyed the parade of sunburned tourists, surfers, vagrants, and street hustlers with myna birds on their shoulders that sauntered by, feeling sweat bead on my forehead in the cool morning air. Herman mumbled something about "an RSP and a Charlie Berman."

With the ease of a man waiting in line at the Department of Motor Vehicles, I explained to Freya that "RSP stands for Red Sea Pedestrians—Jews. You know, Moses leading his people across the Red Sea."

Freya looked lost.

"Charlie Berman is the cockney rhyme for German."

"I have no problem with Jews," she said.

"I know," I said. "Herman just wishes he was Jewish."

Now she looked confused *and* annoyed. I make it a point never to say, "Just kidding," but in this case it might have helped. Herman leaned back, smiling.

The next morning when Freya joined us, Herman added a few Zulu phrases into the passive-aggressive mix. By the end of the week I was slipping out the back of the hotel to have coffee by myself.

Freya had told me that one reason her marriage with her son's father broke up was because he was so uncommunicative. And yet during the many hours we spent together killing time between training sessions, I couldn't get anything like a conversation going. She wasn't interested in current events, history, or me. Although her grandfather fought for the "Charlie Bermans" in World War II and I had relatives who died in concentration camps, we covered the full range of social, geopolitical, and psychological issues surrounding this cataclysmic event in roughly two minutes. "I don't get involved in that stuff," she said, concluding our brief conversation.

One day we were walking down Waikiki when we stopped before a bronze statue of Duke Paoa Kahinu Mokoe Hulikohola Kahanamoku posed before a towering surfboard, welcoming visitors with open arms. The father of modern surfing, Duke stands with his broad back to the beach, his outstretched arms hung with fresh leis placed there by visitors paying homage to Hawaii's greatest waterman. I had been to Duke's canoe club and seen the memorabilia and photos of this perfect specimen. He was 6'1" and 190 pounds, and he had smooth brown skin, dark, penetrating eyes, and thick, slicked-back hair. Having done some research on the topic in the past, I launched into what I thought was a decent lecture on the history of Hawaiian water culture, from the Polynesians who first ventured across the uncharted ocean ten thousand years ago in open, double-hulled sailing canoes to Tom Selleck paddling a surf ski in the opening montage of *Magnum PI*. "Duke distilled the essence of that ancient sailing tradition down to just one man, a piece of polished wood, and the power of the ocean," I said. "He's worshipped here."

I didn't get quite the response I had hoped for. "I don't know him," Freya said.

"He was also an incredible swimmer. Back in 1890 when he was born, it was the local custom for fathers to take their baby sons out in an outrigger and toss them into the surf to teach them how to swim."

"This is a good way to learn."

"Duke won swimming medals in three Olympics. In 1924 he finished second to Johnny Weissmuller."

From her blank expression it appeared she had never heard of Weissmuller. "You know, the guy who played Tarzan?" I said.

Still nothing. "The TV show. 'Me, Tarzan. You, Jane'!" I even did the vine-swinging yell, drawing a few stares from Duke pilgrims passing by but nary a chuckle from Freya. "You saw Tarzan when you were a kid, didn't you?"

"My parents didn't own a TV until I was fourteen years old," she said.

I was striking out big time. Frustrated and feeling unappreciated, I vowed not to speak again until spoken to. But being a gabby RSP from Brooklyn, I broke down minutes later and told her the tale of Duke losing his right index finger fighting a 10-foot eel. And, no, she was not impressed.

Each morning a group of us drove north up the winding, scenic coastal road, led by Oscar Chalupsky. Oscar served as the unofficial coach and tour leader for the younger South African paddlers and anyone else willing to sign on as a supplicant to the living legend of Molokai. Oscar has earned that status fairly, having arrived for the first time back in 1983, a trash-talking twenty-year-old on a mission to supplant Aussie Grant Kenny as the king of the Molokai channel. Bronzed, blue-eyed Kenny was a celebrity in his water-sports-crazed country. He had won Molokai three times in a row and his picture was on cereal boxes. Oscar not only beat him, but he trimmed eleven minutes off his record and then went on to win the race for the next seven years, stopping only when South African athletes were banned from international competition. After a five-year absence, he won four more. He *owned* Molokai.

While maintaining a full racing schedule, Oscar became a partner in Epic Kayaks, a paddle and boat manufacturing concern established by Greg Barton. They were talking with Freya about sponsoring her Australia trip, so Freya was under Oscar's umbrella. On our first training session, Oscar dropped Freya and me off at a car park by a wide, scenic bay called Hawaii Kai, once an ancient fish pond (now the backdrop to a sprawling shopping mall), to do a shorter, less raucous paddle than the one he had planned for himself and the young guns. "Look after Freya," he shouted as he drove off.

We paddled out through the channel markers for twenty minutes to Portlock, where the water crashes off the sheer cliffs, and then turned downwind toward the hulking profile of Diamond Head, an extinct volcano that resembles the brow of a giant tuna, en route to the Outrigger Canoe Club. I was not thrilled with the assignment of minding a slower paddler, but after months of training on a frigid bay in Brooklyn it was pure bliss to get out on the water without an arsenal of gear. The wind and swell rebounded off the rocks with a symphonic roar, the turquoise water exploding into a frothy white spray. For a while I even had an escort of dolphins.

When I looked around, however, Freya was nowhere in sight. I turned into the wind, unsteady in the 6-foot chop, and scanned the horizon for a paddler dressed in black on an invisible white boat. Just whitecaps as far as the eye could see. I bobbed in place like a wobbly cork for what felt like forever until she finally appeared. I felt virtuous for waiting. She felt aggrieved. "A sea kayaker would never leave another sea kayaker out there!"

The implication being, of course, that sea kayakers and surf ski paddlers inhabit different moral universes. And to some extent, they do. The two craft are descended from very different ancestors. Today's sea kayak evolved in a straight line from the Inuit's working boat, which was designed for the serious business of keeping its owner alive in frigid waters while out hunting food for his family. As they say in Greenland, seals don't grow on trees. The surf ski, on the other hand, evolved from the paddleboards used by Australian lifeguards for rescues. That's pretty serious, too, but during all those hours when the lifeguards weren't using the boats to save swimmers they used them to race each other downwind, catching waves like seated surfers, linking the runs like snow skiers in a mogul field. Sea kayaks are not about speed; in fact, by clinging to the traditional Greenland-style hull shape—with an elevated prow to facilitate landing on ice—many of the modern kayaks are slower than they need to be. On the other hand, with no place to store even a sandwich and a pair of binoculars, surf skis are virtually useless for more than a four-hour paddle.

The difference between sea kayakers—tough, hardy, responsible, nature-loving, gearhead loners—and surf ski paddlers—beach bums, heading out with only a Speedo and zinc block—was a theme Freya and I would return to many times. With her balance and strength, Freya very quickly became a competent ski paddler. But the zeitgeist of ski paddling was something she had no interest in mastering.

—————

We met up with Oscar at the genteel, open-aired lanai at the Outrigger Club for lunch. Oscar, already talking, sat down across from Freya. He was still wired from the morning's training and wanted to make clear the difference in the conditions we each had faced—and to be congratulated for his wisdom in sending us on an easy run. Evidently, conditions out at Makapu had been huge. A mile off shore, Zsolt Szadovszki, a Hungarian living in Hawaii, had been cleaned off his ski by a wave three stories high. ("It was a monster," he told me later, his eyes as wide as an owl in need of Visine, half amused and totally in awe.) My little spat with Freya may have put a damper on my paddle, but I was grateful I hadn't had to run the gauntlet on my first day out. I was in the middle of saying so when Freya said she would have been fine with either run. Oscar leaned in and looked her in the eye. "You'd have shat your pants," he said, articulating each word.

"Not so, so why do you think so?"

"You've never been in such violent conditions," he said.

"I have, in New Zealand."

"That is bullshit!" Oscar barked. "These were 50-foot faces!"

"Impossible, Oscar," she replied. "You're exaggerating. Or you don't know how to measure. That's a common problem with men, especially when they talk about their own equipment!"

It was actually good theater, especially if you were a fan of *The Sopranos*. Freya and Oscar were cut from the same cloth. Both are tall, big-boned, powerful figures in their mid-forties—alpha types, with polarizing personalities, who would far rather express an opinion than ask for one. And neither gave a shit about offending the other. One key difference, however, is that Oscar embellished every detail of his life, whereas Freya related her adventures without ever using an adjective (other than *sexy*). Nothing was ever wild, scary, or intense; nothing of consequence ever turned out other than the way it was meant to be. In short, nothing fazed her. While she may have been less colorful than Oscar, she was 98 percent more reliable.

On her two previous expeditions, Freya used a classic British-style boat favored by most expedition sea kayakers. Oscar began building boats before he hit puberty. To him, the classic upturned bow and stern designed by the Inuit was "absolutely useless" for long-distance touring—like driving a Model T across the country. "Use that boat for your Australia trip," he told her during their first meeting, "and it will take you twice as long."

The Epic brand was firmly entrenched with the racing crowd, but had struggled to make inroads with the sea kayaking crowd. Freya liked Epic, liked Greg Barton, and perhaps even recognized a kindred can-do spirit in Oscar. Her biggest concern was whether they would modify their production kayak to the specifications she deemed essential for such a punishing journey. Their primary concern was more practical: Would she live long enough to help sell their boats? Her daily pow-wows with Oscar were part sparring match, part audition.

This lunch was no different. While Freya had two record-setting expeditions on her resume to Oscar's none, that didn't stop him from telling her what gear she should take and what she could afford to leave behind—advice she said she intended to ignore. ("Of course I must take a laptop. This is not a caveman expedition.") But when she turned the conversation to modifications to the boat, he was just as dismissive. She said she needed a retractable skeg. Oscar was outraged. "Why would you compromise the integrity of the boat with a useless feature like that?" he said.

"For when I launch off the beach backwards," she said.

He recoiled as if he'd gulped curdled cream. "That's the stupidest thing I've heard in my life," he said, and graphically described what would happen if she tried such a maneuver in big, dumping surf: The boat would be reduced to rubble, she would break her neck, or both. (You would almost think he had tried it once himself.) When he took a call on his cell phone, she turned to me and, barely lowering her voice, called him a "big pampered boy in a little light boat who wouldn't last a week in a self-supported expedition."

It seems funny to me now, but I remember wishing at the time that the race was over so I could get the hell out of paradise.

Before long most everyone in the paddling crowd had an opinion on the Woman in Black and voiced it whenever she wasn't around. The real source of the mounting social tension was the audacity of her plan, and the lack of humility with which she approached it. Perhaps if she was one of *them*, with a pedigree in lifesaving, surfing, or ski paddling (or was even just an Olympic-caliber flat-water paddler), the Aussie contingent would have given her more credit. A notoriously sexist breed, they might also have been less outraged if *she* had been a *he*. It might even have helped a little if she hailed from some country other than the one that forced nearly a million Australians into World War II. But this big, tough, German sheila, who lacked humility and a sense of humor, got their collective goat in the worst way, and the attacks seemed personal. Correction: The attacks *were* personal. She was called a freak, insane, mad, even shark bait. Some said she had a death wish. Women, in particular, were outraged that she would leave her twelve-year-old son for a year. It didn't help when I told them she hadn't made that decision lightly, that the boy spent most of his time with her ex-husband anyway, and that she had cried when we first talked about it.

She got plenty of unsolicited advice—warnings, actually. A spear fisherman from Sydney told her how tiger sharks would emerge like ghosts from the inky depths to steal massive fish he had caught and strung on a line, passing invisibly within yards of him in the water. A pony-tailed surfer from Peterborough said that the great whites plucked surfers from the Southern Ocean like maraschino cherries from an ice-cream sundae. (Sadly, a few months after Molokai, he went for a paddle in Murnanes Bay, east of Warrnambool, and was never seen again, although his kayak, life jacket, hat, and mobile phone were found.) She heard that one bite from a taipan, the most poisonous snake on the planet, produces enough venom to kill one hundred adults. Then on the west coast there were boat-breaking "bombies"—15-foot breaking waves, far off shore, which stacked up over reefs. Up north, you had the "salties." Illegal hunting put saltwater crocodiles on the endangered list back in the 1970s, after which time the world's largest reptiles began reproducing like saltwater bunnies. The males, which can reach 23 feet and nearly 3,000 pounds, patrol their territory like members of the Hell's Angels, attacking anything that moves, from wallabies to horses lapping at billabongs.

Grant Kenny's father, Hayden, was Freya's loudest critic. A legendary surfer and lifesaver—in 1966 he won the first Australian Ironman Open title at the National Surf Lifesaving Championship—the man we called "Fossil" had a full head of white hair and piercing blue eyes in a craggy, tanned face. Aussie to the core, Fossil had worked in marine rescue for three decades and was positively offended by what he saw as Freya's hubris and ignorance. "She doesn't know what she's getting into," he told me. "Australia is a bastard of a place. Everything wants to kill you, even the sun, and nobody lives along most of the coastline. Assuming you can find a place to land, you can't walk for help because there's nothing for hundreds, if not thousands, of miles. You will just have to march or die. Everyone worries about the crocs up north, but the box jellyfish is responsible for more deaths in Australia than sharks, snakes, and crocs combined. You might be able to stay out of the crocs' way, but how are you going to avoid a jellyfish?"

I passed along the gist of his remarks to Freya, thinking she might want to sit down with him, brainstorm, and get his take on the trip. But she was equally offended by Fossil's remarks. "He is a hateful, negative man. I don't need to hear that kind of talk," she said.

For the first week I played the role of mediator between Freya and the Angry Aussies of Little Faith. She had a right to go and they had legitimate reasons to warn her not to. One afternoon, after a long session with Fossil and a few other AAs of LF, I was convinced that Freya's chances of dying were so great that I had a moral obligation to try to dissuade her. Rather than list the risks, which she didn't want to hear about, I tried to get her to talk about why she wanted to go. Maybe another, less perilous, trip would serve her ends, or another activity entirely.

She just wanted to go, she said, and didn't see why she needed a reason, or cause. She welcomed all challenges. Her strength was problem-solving, in finding a solution at the point where others fail. "The only thing that will stop me," she said, "is serious injury or the death of my son's father. There are hazards to overcome for sure, but basically it's just another trip."

In other words, "*Vasdaproblum?*"

When I told Dean Gardiner what she said he shook his head. At fifteen, Deano dropped out of high school and went to sea on the north coast of Oz. A professional fisherman, boat captain, lifesaver, and paddling legend, he knew the Australian waters as well as anyone. He had just two words on the subject: "She'll die."

But, like a boxer who feeds off his opponent's pre-fight trash-talk, Freya used the negativity and hostility to harden her resolve. Yes, others had tried and failed, but if Paul Caffyn could do it, she could too. So what if he'd had a land crew follow him and she planned to go unsupported. She had been studying his meticulous book and would learn from his mistakes. With a GPS and satellite phone she'd be able to get detailed marine forecasts and avoid the most dangerous days. She'd have a faster kayak and a better paddle. And that's why she would not only complete the trip, but break his record in the process.

Race day came at last. Freya opted to make the crossing in a sea kayak—the one she planned to use around Australia. She finished in six hours and fifteen minutes, second from last,* beating one of the five other women who competed—a tad more than two and a half hours behind Tahitian Lewis Laughlin, who won his second title in Hawaii. More fuel for the naysayers and another reason for her to seek victory in Australia, in her kind of competition.

Her parting words to me: "After I finish I want to return during Molokai and give the finger to everyone who bet against me."

---

* To be fair, she was ahead of six world-class racers who dropped out.

CHAPTER TWO

Leaving the Grey Town by the Sea

Yes, I'll do it. Paddle around Australia. In a kayak. Solo. Unsupported.
Starting this year.
—MISSION STATEMENT FREYA POSTED ON HER BLOG ON
MARCH 12, 2008

A WHO'S WHO OF HUSUM, GERMANY, READS LIKE THIS: KING ABEL OF
Denmark, who was killed in Husum in 1252 after usurping his brother's
throne; the organist Nicolaus Bruhns, an important influence on Bach
and a Husum resident from 1689 to 1697; Theodor Storm, an obscure
nineteenth-century writer who called Husum the "grey town by the sea";
and Freya Hoffmeister, who in 2009 was about to embark on one of the
boldest expeditions in sea kayaking history.

As soon as she returned to her hometown from Hawaii in late May,
Freya got busy preparing for the trip that every Aussie she had met said
was impossible. In fact, by the time she arrived back in Husum she found
this foreboding post waiting for her on her blog, courtesy of someone
calling himself Australian Waterman:

Do your homework. No, really do your homework. I have paddled
and surfed most beaches in this country and you are a complete fool
if you think you can paddle around Australia without being killed.
The crocs up North will eat you. The thousands of kilometers of cliffs
with no landing areas down south will see you either eaten by a
great white or smashed by 40-foot southerly freezing swells. Get a

grip and go do something else. You don't really need to prove yourself this badly do you?

Freya may have wished for a bluebottle jellyfish to get stuck in his shorts, but she didn't take the time to reply. She planned to leave from Perth, Australia, in October, which meant she had just five months to secure sponsors, update her website, book flights, test gear, set up food drops, make contacts along the route, arrange for boat transport, trim 125 topo maps to fit into the clear plastic case that would sit on the deck of her kayak, do some research on avoiding sharks and "salties," organize her business, pay bills, cancel her car insurance, and—well, her to-do list was nearly as long as the instruction manual for the Room Tidying Robot in the Hammacher Schlemmer catalogue. In her leisure time she read Eric Stiller's *Keep Australia on Your Left* and re-read Caffyn's *The Dreamtime Voyage*. She perused trip reports on the web and began corresponding with local paddlers. She hounded Greg Barton, making sure her new expedition boat would be ready in time. "This work is never finished," she wrote on her blog. The only thing she didn't do in the months leading up to her trip was paddle. That's right, she trained not a lick—no paddling, running, or gym work, nada. The way she saw it, she would have plenty of time to paddle once she got to Australia.

Most normal humans would find preparing for a year-long voyage around a continent they had never seen a daunting undertaking, especially when some of the decisions—for example, whether or not to take a desalinator—could have grave consequences. But, meticulous and detail-oriented, Freya is at her best when she's organizing *something*. Even when she kicks back, she finds problems to solve. She spent three months completing a ten-thousand-piece jigsaw puzzle of the New York City skyline. And she had her eye on a mural by the graffiti artist Keith Haring billed as "the world's largest puzzle" with thirty-two thousand pieces.

She started organizing things at an early age. She quit college to work as the manager of Janny's Eis, an ice-cream shop, living above it in a tiny apartment overlooking the North Sea. At twenty-three, she bought the franchise with an inheritance she received from a forgotten uncle on her father's side. Five years later she had six more. Today she owns only two, but with a well-trained staff of forty women (most of them young and pretty, she told me) you can bet your chocolate-covered hazelnuts that the line moves efficiently even on the hottest days in this bustling port town.

After the tourists leave for the summer, Freya transforms one of her stores into a Christmas shop. She stocks the shelves with more than five thousand trinkets and ornaments—sometimes working for thirty-six hours nonstop—placing each item in just the right spot, like jewelry in a display case. "If it becomes messy," she said, "it becomes crazy." Unlike most of us, Freya does not put off for tomorrow what she can do today. Give her a task and she's as focused as a beaver paid by the dam.

Perhaps the most time-consuming part of her trip preparations was chasing sponsors, but Freya saw this as more of a sport than a chore. Because she had only recently returned from her paddle around New Zealand's South Island, she really didn't need much in terms of gear. Having a long list of sponsors was more about validation, about being professional—and she just plain enjoyed the challenge of luring hip companies onto her website.

In August, a few months after Molokai, she flew to Salt Lake City for the Outdoor Retailer Show, the world's biggest gathering of active lifestyle manufacturers, for what amounted to a sponsor safari. Her home base was the Epic Kayaks booth, manned by Greg Barton, but she spent most of her time cruising the show in a shiny black neoprene ensemble custom-made by Reed Chillcheater. Amidst the ubiquitous jeans, baggy shorts, and crocs, she stood out like Pat Benatar on steroids in a zip-front dress opened to halfway up her thigh and a tight jacket that brought the eye to the bone necklace at her throat. She wore her shades atop her curly black hair and strutted her stuff in 4-inch, open-toed black heels—in a word, she was fabulous. Any man under 6 feet tall needed to be secure in his manhood to have his picture taken with her. Freya greeted dozens of potential sponsors, pitching her project with a brilliant smile, secure in the knowledge that her trip was badass to the core. Once back in Husum, she fanned the business cards that interested her across the kitchen table, tossed the rest, and started e-mailing proposals.

There was also ample work to do on the home front. One of her biggest concerns, naturally enough, was leaving her shops for a year, but after a few meetings with her most capable managers she had that sorted out. Then there was her house, her car, and her RV, which she planned to ask her ex-husband to look after. He was a retired Navy Kampfschwimmer—a commando frogman, similar to a US Navy SEAL—and the kind of guy who can parachute at night behind enemy lines, repair a car engine, prepare a nutritionally balanced meal, and change a mean diaper, all with perfect posture. Freya felt confident that he would agree to assume full-time care of their twelve-year-old son, but as far as Werner doing her any extra favors . . . well, it was complicated.

For the record, Werner was Freya's second husband. It took a while for me to learn the story of her first husband, a tall, strong, "very sexy" pilot named Frank who walked into her ice-cream shop in the summer of 1986. In just a few weeks they were living together. Three years later, they had a "big fancy wedding" and moved into a house Freya had bought. But they had barely unpacked the dishes when Frank took off with one of her employees.

Ouch.

Freya told me she can't remember if she was surprised that he left after just three months of marriage; then she added "I don't want to remember." His problem, she insisted, was he always wanted to be a pilot in the German air force and that required him, oddly enough, to study in the United States. He needed a wife to go with him. "I wasn't such a woman!"

After Frank left, Freya began spending most of her free time jumping out of airplanes. She did three hundred jumps in her first few years and was in Hamburg, training to get a tandem pilot's license, when an instructor named Werner Wuerger, a decorated military man with more than fifteen hundred jumps, caught her eye. At forty-eight, he was eighteen years her senior. "I looked up to him," she said. "Not size-wise, but experience-wise." He was balding and a bit shorter than Freya—not ideal in her book—but he had a chest as thick as a slab of beef and a pair of powerful shoulders. Freya said, with a chuckle, "He was attracted to my ass; I was attracted to his tits. He was solid muscle."

Two weeks later, Werner moved in, bringing his seven-year-old son from a previous marriage.

It was romance commando-style. "We were always fighting," she said. About what, she can't recall, but she chalks it up to the stars. "I'm a Taurus. I love to be wooed and romanced. He's an Aries, straightforward, brash, unsubtle." Her first husband was a Gemini, which she also said was bad. Surprising, I thought, that someone as logical and precise as Freya would rely on astrology to explain a failed relationship—but, after all, relationships are complicated. The most concrete explanation she gave was, "I'm an extremely positive person and with Werner everything is negative." She paused, adding, "But he calls it being realistic."

One wonders if Werner had reason to be negative. Three years into their relationship, on a trip to the North Pole to set a record for the largest group jump over the northern-most point on Earth, the furtive glances Freya exchanged with the handsome cameraman were not lost on the career Navy man trained in surveillance. Tensions ran so high that she considered cashing in the one for the other on the spot. "I was flirting too much," she said, "but I didn't want to be with him anymore. I liked being independent and wanted to get away somehow."

Freya and Werner completed the jump and went home together, but a pattern had been set. It's worth mentioning that after Freya's father died in 1993, she discovered a stack of love letters from a number of women hidden in the cellar of the family home. This surprised her not at all. "My father was tall and strong, good-looking and charming," she said. "All you need for a man." Freya had spent many happy days in the woods hunting with her father and wasn't speaking metaphorically when she said: "He was a hunter and I'm a hunter. I like to flirt and to hunt. But if I'm happy in a relationship, holding myself back is much easier."

The fact that Werner already had a son was also hard on the relationship. "I did lots of things for Christian," she said, "but I always felt in the way." As her inclination to leave grew stronger, Werner became more possessive, and as his trust eroded things went increasingly sour. "I wasn't flirting in secret," she said, "I told him that I wasn't happy. It wasn't a good thing for me to do but if I was happy with Werner, I'd not have flirted with other men. That's simply the way it is."

And yet they decided to have a child. Was it to save the relationship, or because she wanted a child? "Both, from my side," she said. "It
shouldn't be like that, I know. But we agreed to give it a try. It took two
years from stopping the pill and one miscarriage to get Helge."

Freya was thirty-one years old when she got pregnant. She had been
skydiving for a decade. She loved the free-floating feeling of flight and
the sense of risk each time she stepped into thin air above 14,000 feet,
knowing she was truly on her own. The pressure of air against her body
allowed her to move like an aerial gymnast for as much as a minute before
she had to deploy her chute. She had jumped from as high as 21,325
feet and been towed behind a plane in a kind of horizontal freefall that
lasted half an hour. "The higher and longer the better," she said. But facts
were facts: Ten of her colleagues, many of them highly experienced, had
died skydiving. When she learned she was pregnant, soon after her fifteen
hundredth jump, she hung up her chute for good.

In January 1996 Helge Hoffmeister was born.* Freya threw herself
wholeheartedly into motherhood, carrying her son in a sling wherever she
went. Werner had introduced her to kayaking after she stopped skydiving,
and she started taking Helge out with her when he was just six months old,
sitting in the back hatch of her folding sea kayak with a custom-made spray
skirt. She paddled for hours with her "happy little man." In the early days,
he mostly napped; as he got older, he'd sit tucked behind her broad back as
she paddled alongside another paddler and blast away with his water pistol.

Freya and Werner married when Helge was two, "for tax reasons," she
said. But as much as each parent loved the child, Helge's presence was
another wedge between them. Freya has always been a loner; she calls herself a "one-on-one person." Growing up, she wasn't close to her mother or
sister, only her father, and she has never had a girlfriend ("I never missed
having one and I never looked for one," she said). Given the difficulties in
her relationship with Werner, once Helge arrived on the scene, he became
the one. "My husband was not my real partner. That was my son."

---

* Freya says that the couple decided Helge would take her name because Werner's surname, Wuerger,
means "strangle" in German.

But Werner, according to Freya, is also a one-on-one kind of guy. As Freya became more serious about paddling, she drove around Europe to kayaking symposiums in the 25-foot Niesmann & Bischoff motor home she bought with an inheritance from her grandmother. With her background in gymnastics, it wasn't long before she'd mastered the rolls that are integral to the sport. After just three summers she was a featured guest at these very same symposiums. To a hard-charging Taurus stuck in a passionless relationship, life in Husum was all work and precious little play. On the road she found freedom, a modicum of fame, and, more importantly, the possibility of love . . . or at least a good romp in her RV. But the farther and more often she traveled, the more she relied on Werner to handle the parenting and the further she drifted away from her son.

When Helge was eight, Werner moved to a house less than half a mile away. Freya had never spoken to him about the other men in her life but feels certain that somehow he knew. As the years passed, Freya and Werner negotiated an uneasy peace. In 2007 she was away for nearly four months for her trips around Iceland and the South Island of New Zealand. Werner, she said, seemed only too happy to have Helge to himself. I didn't interview Werner, so I only know Freya's side of the story but, as she tells it, they couldn't do the job of raising their son together. Freya *had* to leave Husum and Werner *had* to stay to take care of Helge. Children typically have a thing for consistency, and Helge chose to make his father's home his primary residence.

When at last she approached the taciturn Kampfschwimmer with her plan to paddle around Australia, he was supportive. She was surprised at first, but then decided she had it figured out. "He was happy that I was going away as I would be no longer taking any of his time away from Helge." After a pause, she added, "This is at least what I was sensing."

And—perhaps to remove any impediment to her going?—Werner also said he would take good care of her house, garden and all the rest.

Freya's original departure date of October had to be postponed to January when operations at the Epic factory in China came to a grinding halt.

The dispute between Epic and their manufacturer, a company called Flying Eagle, is a long story and not one that needs to be told here, but by December it became obvious that the standoff would continue and the boat that Freya requested wouldn't be ready by the first of the year. Not a good omen. Greg Barton suggested she fly to Sydney in January, pick up a production boat from the dealer there, drive a rental car to Melbourne, and start as planned.

Though Freya understood that the problem was beyond Epic's control, the delay irritated her immensely. She had 9,000 miles to paddle, and if she started much after the first of the year she would reach the notoriously rough Southern Ocean in the winter when it was far more dangerous. At the same time, using a "flimsy" production boat could prove disastrous if the surf in Australia was anything like what she had experienced circling New Zealand's South Island. Paddling a durable British-designed three-piece sea kayak there, a wave on the west coast picked her up and pounded her on the rocky shore so hard that it dislocated the back end of her kayak like a pinky finger.

Freya deliberated for a week. She had put much thought into the modifications she needed and spent a fair amount of time negotiating them with Epic, and she had serious concerns about using the production model. After more than a few disgruntled e-mails to Greg, they agreed on a compromise: She would start in the production boat and when the modified boat was ready Epic would somehow get it to her en route. She let him know that she was already living up to her end of the deal—promoting the Epic brand—and that it was high time for him to do the same.

On January 11, 2009, Freya woke before her alarm sounded. At 3:30 a.m. she tossed three heavy duffel bags into the back seat of her rental car, cranked the heat, and drove out of her grey town by the North Sea. It was less than a two-hour drive to the airport in Hamburg, but Freya had been going full tilt the last week and had to pull over twice to nap. She turned on the radio, smiling when she heard "Burning Heart," the theme song from *Rocky IV*. Her good-bye with Helge kept replaying in her mind, much as she tried not to think about it. She had left home many times before, so maybe it wasn't so surprising that he should treat this good-bye like those others—no big deal. Certainly she had done nothing to upset him; she kept her tears to herself. But Helge seemed almost unaware that she was heading off for twelve months and that her journey would be a dangerous one.

Of the many criticisms I have heard of Freya's trip, her decision to leave her son for a year, perhaps never to return, has drawn the harshest attacks. I have a daughter the same age as Helge, and I understand that the need to chase a dream that takes you far from home, and even into danger, doesn't go away when you have a child. And when the adventurer is a woman people tend to chirp louder. I was reminded of Alison Hargreaves, the first woman to solo Everest without supplemental oxygen. Generally considered the best female alpinist in history, Hargreaves had two young children and when she announced that she aimed to climb K2, the world's second-tallest mountain and one that claims a higher percentage of climbers than Everest, she was roundly criticized. On August 13, 1995, she reached the summit, becoming the first woman to climb both peaks without supplemental oxygen. On the descent a storm swept her off the mountain, and her body was never found. The criticism sounded all over again.

So, how does a mother justify the risk of leaving her child motherless? Although Freya was clearly uncomfortable with this line of questioning, I kept after her. Finally, she cut me off mid-sentence. "Sure, I like to travel," she said, "but the reason I travel so much is Helge. Saying good-bye is hard, but sitting at home all alone while Helge is down the road is worse. It's horrible sitting by myself, more or less lonely, when he's so near." And then, for once, she filled the awkward silence. "No one who is paddling around Australia is happy at home."

When interviewers ask her the inevitable question, why paddle around Australia, Freya generally responds with some version of "Because it is there." In a rare show of vulnerability, she had provided another answer: "Because it isn't here."

Chapter Three

A Journey of 9,420 Miles Begins with a Single Sticker

Amongst sea kayakers Paul Caffyn is almost in a class of his own. For the longest time after he finished his awesome solo circumnavigation of Australia the silence was deafening: few of his peers knew the significance of what he had done, and perhaps those who understood felt lost in his shadows. Not only is Paul's Australian adventure a pinnacle for sea kayaking, it should eventually be recognized as one of the great small voyages of recent history along with those of Slocum, Shackleton and Franz Romer.
—John Dowd, author of Sea Kayaking: A Manual for Long Distance Touring

After a delay in London, a layover in Singapore and another eight restless hours crammed in the middle seat in the last aisle of a jumbo jet, Freya arrived in Sydney at 10:00 p.m. on January 11, 2009. She was jetlagged and, worse, short one equipment bag packed with essential paddling gear. Tony King, the Epic agent in Sydney, met her at the airport, but because he and his wife Jacqui were leaving town early the next morning he had booked her a room in a quaint hotel within shouting distance of the harbor. Though King paid for the room, Freya made it clear she wasn't happy: She doesn't like hotels and prefers to stay with "the people" when she travels. Said Freya: "I felt a bit like an unwanted parcel."

She turned off the AC and opened a window to the muggy night air. Unable to sleep, she stayed up writing in her blog. "I hate air conditioning as much as hot humid nights, but I still chose the latter to get used to. There won't be air conditioning in my tent, although on the beach with some breeze it might be much nicer than in this hotel room."

Early the next morning, Freya walked to the suburb of Manly Beach and joined the throng of tanned runners, iPod-wearing cyclists and toned moms with baby joggers on the pedestrian path that hugs the coast. Even at 6:30 a.m., the ocean was busy with swimmers, surfers, and surf ski paddlers heading out to sea. Staring out at the lines of head-high surf rolling toward the beach, she pictured trying to get through the shore break—and three additional lines of breakers beyond that—in her fully loaded kayak. *Welcome to Australia, mate.*

She would have loved to have gone for a swim, but her bathing suit was in her missing bag. "I was a bit late for a decent skinny-dip," she wrote on her blog. I mention this because it was the first of 167 references to her own full or partial nudity she would post in the coming months. The second followed right behind: "But I guess I will be dipping enough the whole next year. ☺"

Freya spent the day with Dale Ponsford, an Epic employee, who drove her around Sydney as she changed money, got her cell phone running, retrieved her missing bag, and did some shopping. With sun-bleached hair and chilled *fucking-A, mate* attitude, Ponsford was literally born to surf. His father was one of the Torquay Board riders, a band of surfing mates who "discovered" Bells Beach,* 60 miles southwest of Melbourne. Dale started surfing when he was five and is also an avid paddler and a spear fisherman; in other words, he is well acquainted with the Southern Ocean. That morning, he greeted Freya a bit warily; in his mind, she was a dead woman walking. "I didn't think that she would make it—nobody did," he wrote to me. "I was concerned for her safety doing long exposed stretches in bad weather."

After a day in her company, though, he put her chances at better than zero. "I realized that she was incredibly strong-willed, focused, and

---

* Bells Beach appears in the 1966 documentary *The Endless Summer* and is home to the world's longest-running surfing competition.

determined. She didn't see failure as an option. I kind of figured if anyone could do it, it would be her."

While they tooled around town, another Epic-Oz man, Andrew Divola, worked to retool Freya's Epic sea kayak. As per her instructions, he installed a third bulkhead and day hatch, reinforced the hull, and shored up the seat and bow toggle. Not surprisingly, Freya completed her tasks before he had finished his; she commented on her blog that she would have to lose her German habit of efficiency and "switch to BIG ISLAND time."

Finally, after the third day in the shop with Divola, gluing, fiberglassing, painting, and adding loops and bungees and netting in the cockpit to store everything she would need for the days she planned to spend at sea, she was ready for the long drive to Melbourne. Her blog entry at the end of the day was vintage Freya, titillating and straightforward both: "Dusty and dirty as I was, and with pants fully torn on my backside, I hurried to get started. No pictures . . . and yes, I'm fat right now." With a smiley face, of course.

On Thursday morning, she rented a car downtown, opting not to pay extra for the kangaroo collision insurance. She scanned Sydney's magnificent harbor as she passed it by and felt a pang of regret, but reminded herself that she was on a mission, not a sightseeing tour. Driving southwest away from the coast, she cruised through 539 miles of dry, featureless landscape made marginally more exciting by the signs warning motorists about koalas, wallabies, and (*oh, shit!*) kangaroos. By 2:00 she could barely keep her eyes open. It was broiling outside—104 in the shade. To catch some shut-eye she had to leave the engine running to use the despised AC.

While she passed plenty of "flattish, furry piles" along the Hume Highway, she herself had no encounters with the native fauna and made it from Sydney, Australia's biggest city, to Melbourne, the second biggest, in thirteen hours. Her trip suddenly seemed very near.

In 1802 a British skipper named John Murray sailing the Southern Ocean made his way through treacherous water between two headlands into a shallow, heart-shaped bay. He may have been the first European to explore the massive bay he dubbed Port Phillip, but when he arrived there were fifteen thousand Aborigines living off the fat of the land (specifically, the fat of seals and penguins). Judging from the semi-fossilized shell middens left behind, they were also early raw-bar enthusiasts. The Brits soon returned with three hundred convicts to establish a settlement, but although the area had been inhabited for at least thirty thousand years before Queen Elizabeth's reign, they couldn't find enough food or fresh water and left after a year. Other Europeans arrived overland from Sydney, but for most of the next forty years Melbourne was more of a distant outpost than a viable city. Then gold was discovered in 1851 and the white population exploded, with predictable results for the natives. By 1880 "Marvelous Melbourne" was one of the richest cities on earth.

By most accounts it's still pretty marvelous, but Freya had no time for Melbourne, either. There was food to buy and sixty pounds of gear to sort and stow. At the risk of sounding like a gear weenie, it's impossible to overstate how important proper packing is to the success of a long expedition, which is, first and foremost, a war of attrition on body, spirit, and equipment. Job one for the paddler is to keep himself or herself as safe, healthy, and comfortable as possible, a difficult task made easier by bringing the right amount of the right gear, keeping it in good working condition, and knowing where to find it.

Freya is a packing genius. Maybe it's a German thing, maybe it's the hundreds of hours she's spent organizing Christmas *tchotchkes* in her shops, but she's got the Right Spot for everything. Into the cockpit went the stuff she would use every day while paddling—food, drink, a funnel-type device for peeing while seated, sunscreen, lip balm, and cell and satellite phones—and stuff she might need—a pump and sponge, flashlight, headlamp, flares, rope, diving knife, and spare batteries. The new day hatch, just behind the cockpit, also held items she might need to get at quickly, like a boat repair kit, first-aid kit, and spare GPS. Strapped on the boat would be her spare paddle, helmet, life jacket (with an EPIRB[*] in the pocket), and her map case, GPS, VHF radio, and camera. The forward and aft hatches,

---

[*] An EPIRB is a small battery-powered transmitting device used only in case of emergency and usually only as a last resort when your marine radio is inoperable or out of range.

which she couldn't reach from the cockpit, held her camping gear, dry clothes, food supplies, laptop, one book (*The Dreamtime Voyage*) and one luxury item: a whisk broom for sweeping sand out of her tent.

Her final task was to place sponsor decals on her pristine white kayak. It took her an entire afternoon, but when she finished her boat looked slick and professional, with more logos than an Indy 500 race car. She had added her own personal touches as well. Up front, in bold black letters, was the name of her venture, RACE AROUND AUSTRALIA 2009, with the slogan ADDICTED TO SPEED. More intriguing, just below the cockpit appeared the words, FREYA SHAKTI.

When Freya paddled around New Zealand she named her boat[*] *Veni, Vidi, Vici*, the phrase made famous by Caesar upon his victory over Pharnaces: "I came, I saw, I conquered." I'm a sucker for a good Latin phrase, so I thought that was pretty cool—but Freya Shakti? It's the name of a song Freya found on iTunes by a kilt-wearing band from Georgia named Emerald Rose, an homage to all female goddesses but especially Freya, the Norse goddess of love, beauty, sex, and war. "Shakti" comes from the Hindu tradition and means sacred force or empowerment. Put the two together, and Freya thought it fit her pretty well.

Now, obviously Freya didn't name herself, but it takes a healthy dose of chutzpah to proclaim oneself the namesake of the goddess of love and beauty. And yet when I consulted Goddessfreya.info and Goddess-Guide.com, I was struck by more than a few similarities:

MYTHIC FREYA: Her beauty was known far and wide (in Scandinavia, anyway) and no man could resist her if she was wearing her enchanted jeweled necklace, which had been made by four dwarves in exchange for spending a night with each of them.

MODERN FREYA: Freya, who won her share of beauty pageants, sported two necklaces in Oz: the Maori pendant I had seen her wearing in San Juan, given to her by an old flame, and a sterling silver kayak from the owner of a kayak shop in Sydney. True, neither of these men is a dwarf.

---

[*] She was paddling a Nigel Dennis boat, the *Explorer*. She modified the name with a big red *S* to read "SExplorer."

MYTHIC FREYA: Although married to the sun god Od, the goddess had many lovers.

MODERN FREYA: Freya's ex-husband Werner, while not technically a god, could fly through the air and breathe underwater, so he might as well have been. As for the lovers, there's a reason Freya cheerfully calls herself a "man eater."

MYTHIC FREYA: The goddess Freya represents an untamable force of nature. She seeks to obtain what she desires and does not take into account the needs of others.

MODERN FREYA: Bingo!

Freya's base for the three days she stayed in Melbourne was the spacious suburban home of Les Bognar, a former president of the Victoria Sea Kayak Club (VSKC), on the eastern shore of Port Phillip Bay. Les and his wife, Anne, hosted a send-off party for Freya on her last night. It was a buffet for sixteen, with the food set out alongside Freya's colorful sea kayak—"my floating billboard," as she fondly referred to it.

Melbourne, which sits on Port Phillip Bay, is 50 miles from the Southern Ocean. In the morning, Bognar loaded Freya's boat on his SUV for the long drive along the shore road to Queenscliff, a sleepy town near the entrance of the bay, where Caffyn started his journey twenty-seven years earlier.

Their first stop on the road was Shortland's Bluff. In 2007 the VSKC unveiled a modest monument dedicated to Paul Caffyn to recognize the twenty-fifth anniversary of his historic trip, a boulder with a plaque that reads:

On the twenty-eighth of December 1981, an Australian-born New Zealand–based adventurer, Paul Caffyn, set out from this Queenscliff beach on the "Dreamtime Voyage," the first solo attempt to circumnavigate the Australian mainland by sea kayak.

LESS THAN ONE YEAR LATER ON THE TWENTY-THIRD OF DECEMBER
1982, PAUL CAFFYN RETURNED TO THIS BEACH AFTER SUCCESSFULLY
COMPLETING HIS 17,400 KILOMETRE VOYAGE.

THIS INCREDIBLE FEAT OF TENACITY AND ENDURANCE EARNED PAUL
CAFFYN HIS PLACE IN HISTORY. MAY HIS ACHIEVEMENT INSPIRE
OTHERS WITH A SPIRIT OF ADVENTURE.

Soon after, Freya posted a photo on her blog taken on her visit to Caffyn Cove. Dressed in her official yellow and black Epic rash guard and paddling shorts, she's sitting demurely on the thigh-high boulder, half a cheek away from the bronze image of Caffyn, the shirtless, rail-thin, bushy-bearded, bespectacled geologist, pushing forward in his Valley Nordkapp sea kayak.

Freya's relationship with the Grand Old Man of Distance Sea Kayaking is a tad complex. Or maybe it's not so complex. They began their friendship in the roles of novice and legend: Freya had contacted Paul before her New Zealand trip in 2008 and he generously shared valuable information and advice. Then, just before setting out, she pinched a nerve in her shoulder and spent three days at his house healing and going over trip details. Freya was sixty days into her paddle when a nasty front moved through. She contacted Caffyn in nearby Greymouth, and he suggested she wait out the storm at his home on the edge of the Tasman Sea. It was Christmas Day. The fire was crackling, the port was flowing, and the opera *Carmen* was on the telly—an altogether cozy break from the rigors of the west coast.

Freya had not yet thought about paddling around Australia—she figured New Zealand's North Island to be next—but Caffyn's amazing journey captured her imagination. She wanted an inscribed copy of *The Dreamtime Voyage*. There was one small glitch: The book was self-published and he only had two copies left on his shelf.

Let's just say that a delicate negotiation ensued, at the end of which Freya got her book. And five days later, after covering the final 102 miles in thirty-two hours, she paddled into Okiwi Bay, becoming just the fourth person and the first woman to solo the treacherous South Island. Caffyn's record of seventy-six days had stood since 1978; Freya finished six days faster. The roles had begun to shift. "Paul tried to keep me at his house as long as possible to make my trip last longer than his," she said—joking, but not really.

If Caffyn was bitter, he certainly didn't show it. He organized a welcoming party, complete with a press helicopter, cake, and champagne. Afterwards, she spent another two weeks with him. But when she e-mailed two months later to tell him she was going to have a crack at Oz—solo and unsupported—his reply was curt. He said that without a support team or, at the very least, a desalinator, she had no chance at making it around. "I don't think he wanted to see someone copying his most precious achievement," she said. "Especially a German and a girl."

Now one of the two dozen well-wishers gathered to see her off, David Golightly, who had commissioned the twenty-fifth anniversary plaque, handed her his cell and suggested she call Caffyn. They had spoken just once in the last year, but when he answered she spoke in her breathiest tones, "Hello, sweetheart. I've been longing to speak to you."

Golightly stepped back as if he had burst into a honeymoon suite without knocking. Freya pressed on, growing more delighted as the staid lads around her grew more uncomfortable. Few of those assembled knew that Freya had decided long ago that she was going to paddle around Australia not only unsupported, but faster than Caffyn had, so they heard the seduction but missed the subtext. "In a silly way, I was telling him, I'm coming after you, so watch out," she told me later. She laughed and added, "I'm a very confident girl."

Before they said their good-byes, Freya asked if he planned to be in Queenscliff when she finished. "No worries," he said. "I'll be at the finish."

It might have been an easy promise for him to make. Remember, he thought an unsupported circumnavigation was impossible.

Chapter Four

Punching the Clock in
Terra Australis Incognita

Australia is properly speaking an island, but it is so much larger than every other island on the face of the globe, that it is classed as a continent in order to convey to the mind a just idea of its magnitude.
—Captain Charles Sturt (1795–1869), English explorer
who led several expeditions to the interior

Most of the nearly seven hundred shipwrecks that have taken place in Port Phillip Bay occurred as boats tried to enter it against a strong ebb tide in an area known as the Rip, a triangular section of water between Point Lonsdale and Point Nepean. It's nearly 2 miles between the points, but the reefs that jut out beneath them constrict the navigable channel to half a mile, and the massive volume of water rushing in and out of the narrow slot creates a current of up to 9 knots. To make conditions still more treacherous, the rocky sea floor just outside the headlands rises and falls as precipitously as a Coney Island roller coaster. This short stretch of water is thought to be one of the most dangerous navigable channels in the world.

Day 1: Sunday, January 18, 2009

Two dozen people accompanied Freya to the beach, including Bognar and fellow VSKC member Peter Treby, who had agreed to mail additional gear and provisions for her to pick up in towns along the way. A bearded man in a floppy hat from the Queenscliffe Maritime Museum stood by with the museum's potent toy cannon.

Freya climbed into her boat at ten in the morning to catch the ebb tide. At her side were Peter Treby and Andrew Ponsford, Dale's brother. Les Bognar chose not to paddle out with her into the raging currents; he saw it as an act of self-preservation. The cannon's explosion made Freya's heart skip a beat, but 2 miles later she tapped through the headlands with the nonchalance of an English lady cantering across a meadow on her favorite mare.

As the hours ticked by, Freya focused on one thing—staying awake. The weeks of preparation, the lost day of travel, the missing luggage, and all the last-minute hassles with her boat had taken their toll, and she was struggling to remain upright. Leaning forward, she rested her head on the deck and, quite literally, drifted off.

Soon she had another problem: The swell, rising and falling like Gulliver's belly, was making her seasick. She assumed it was because she had done so little paddling since returning from Hawaii in May that she had lost her sea legs. In fact, she would battle with seasickness off and on for her entire trip. Once she puked up the last of her high-tech sports drink she felt better, at least for the time being.

She pushed east along the Mornington Peninsula, a scenic beachfront lined with summer homes. Here's an esoteric bit of local color for you: On a December morning in 1967, Harold Holt, then prime minister, was hanging out at his favorite Mornington beach with some friends. Although the beach is notorious for its currents and the surf was thumping that day, Holt plunged into the water against his friends' advice, swam a few hundred feet, and vanished forever. His body was never found. One theory was that he had committed suicide; another that he faked his death to run away with his mistress; another (my favorite), that he had been abducted by a Chinese submarine. But Dale Ponsford had a more grimly realistic explanation: "Anytime you're in the ocean you're part of the food chain." As a spear fisherman, he should know.

Later, Peter Treby told Freya that Andrew Ponsford, who had turned around a few miles past the Heads, was unable to make headway against the pumping current and had to be towed in by a Jet Ski. Another kayaker capsized, was unable to roll or climb back in, and was floundering dangerously in the busy shipping channel before he was pulled out.

Why, I wondered, hadn't Freya described the raucous conditions of her first day of paddling on her blog? "To me this was not worth talking about," she said.

But was she scared? Please. "If I was scared about getting out of such an entrance with some bumpy water I shouldn't even be thinking about paddling around a continent."

Eleven hours after pushing off that morning, she approached the small peninsula that marked her destination for that day. Just off the point, the whoosh of walls of water crashing over a reef snapped her out of her lethargy. She gave the reef a wide birth and made a smooth landing on the same beach where Caffyn had stopped on his first night, twenty-seven years earlier. His book would serve as a blueprint for her trip and—with a few notable exceptions—she followed it scrupulously.

There was a No CAMPING sign posted—Caffyn hadn't mentioned that!—but it was Sunday night and no one was around, and in any case she was too tired to paddle another inch. Freya rinsed off in a frigid outdoor shower and crawled into her tent, sweeping the sand out behind her. Too tired to cook, she nibbled on a handful of cheese crackers and collapsed on her mat. Her feet felt like frozen fish sticks and sleep was slow in coming. But she was 34 miles into her trip and it felt good to be underway at last.

DAY 2: MONDAY, JANUARY 19

It's only fitting that Flinders, a small town on the Mornington Peninsula, would be the first stop for someone paddling around Australia. Matthew Flinders was an Englishman born in the late eighteenth century who read *Robinson Crusoe* as a boy and went to sea at fifteen. He sailed the South Pacific under Captain Bligh and in 1795 helped to chart much of the southern coast of Australia. In 1801, two years before Lewis and Clark set out to find a water route to the Pacific, Flinders began a slow circumnavigation of "Terra Australis Incognita," the unknown southern land. He survived a shipwreck, lost eight members of his crew, and spent some time in a French prison in Mauritius on the way home.

He also produced an impressively accurate map, on which the vast landmass that was now the object of Freya's undivided attention was called, for the first time, Australia.

Upon arising, Freya checked her satellite phone for a weather report sent as a text message from a man known to the rest of us only as "Karel." Living on a kibbutz halfway between Tel Aviv and Haifa, Karel Vissel is a kayaker who gives back to the sport he loves by maintaining a website called "kayakweather.com" with the tagline "Supporting kayak expeditions worldwide." Every day for the next year, he would send Freya a message with the wind direction and speed and the size of the swell. Every night for the next year, she would text her position—her latitude and longitude, as indicated by her GPS—to him before she went to bed. Karel forwarded her message to a small group of support people, including Chris Cunningham, the editor of *Sea Kayaker* magazine, one of her trip sponsors. Cunningham would post a note on her blog to let her followers know where she was.

Freya packed up her tent, her sleeping bag, and her considerable electronic arsenal and left Flinders knowing everything that could be known about the wind, the waves, and the weather up ahead.

DAY 3: TUESDAY, JANUARY 20

Freya started the day paddling into a light headwind, but as the day wore on the wind increased in strength and her boat speed slowed to a crawl. Still, she kept going until she reached her planned take-out, more than 30 miles down the road. She was on the water for over 13 hours and never got out of the boat once.

Freya was not easing into the trip.

That night she discovered an ugly saltwater rash on her torso. "I took some pictures," she wrote on her blog, "but decided to leave them private."

DAY 4: WEDNESDAY, JANUARY 21

Wilsons Promontory, known to locals as "the Prom," is a jumbled pyramid of granite boulders topped with a majestic white lighthouse looking across the Bass Strait to Tasmania. The most southerly point of the

Australian mainland, fifteen thousand years ago it was part of a land bridge to Tassie. As Freya passed by, she thought about getting out to have a look at this "beautiful pile of rocks," but practical considerations won out, as they almost always would for the next year. She had a tailwind and she rode it north to Refuge Cove, covering 40.4 miles in 10.5 hours.

Day 5: Thursday, January 22

For the first time on the trip Freya had to wrestle with more than fatigue.

She was a mile and a half off shore, heading north toward Rabbit Island into a moderate headwind, when the wind stopped as suddenly as if someone had flipped a switch. Ten minutes later it returned with a vengeance, except now it was much stronger—up to 25 mph —and much hotter. It was as if a dragon were trying to blow her out to sea. "The strangest hot wind I'd ever experienced," she said. A prudent person might have called it quits for the day, and she did consider stopping. But using the land as protection, she hugged the headland at the northern end of Wilsons Promontory. After four days of straightforward paddling, she liked the challenge of outsmarting and outmuscling the wind; she found it invigorating.

Then it got worse. The wind doubled in strength, now gusting to 45 mph. But this is how Freya thinks: OK, wind, if you can get stronger, I can get stronger, too. For the next hour she leaned forward like a speed skater rounding a turn. Had her GPS not told her that she was traveling 3 to 4 mph she would have thought she was standing still. It was, she said, "a hard, fighting pleasure. It's all about facing the enemy."

Bashing into the same oven-hot wind early in his journey, a discouraged Paul Caffyn considered throwing in the towel. "If headwinds were to predominate until I reached the southeast trade-wind belt north of Brisbane," he wrote in *The Dreamtime Voyage*, "it could take months to clear the New South Wales coast. Wind was definitely the curse of the canoeing class."

Finally, after covering just 12 miles in 3.5 hours, Freya took out near a river in the shade of a stand of tea trees on a protected beach behind

Johnny Souey Point. Bathing in the cool, dark brown water soothed her sore skin. Unbeknownst to her, the Bundjalung people who had inhabited this area used to inhale the oils from crushed tea tree leaves to treat colds, sore throats, and skin ailments; they also used the leaves to cover wounds. But the moment she stood up, fat, nasty flies and biting ants as big as Raisinets forced her to retreat to her airless tent. First she lay in a pool of sweat; then, as rain began falling in sheets, she found herself freezing. The squall passed, the steamy heat returned, and moments later thousands of little crabs skittered across the sand outside the nylon walls of her tent. She managed to doze off only to be awakened by a squawking parrot getting into it with a chorus of crickets. With the rumble of the surf adding to the disquiet, time passed very slowly that night.

New Zealand had been sterile by comparison. She would have to get used to bush life in Oz.

DAY 6: FRIDAY, JANUARY 23

She had covered 40 miles in 11 hours, and now she sat outside the backline of surf off a beach near the Jack Smith Lake Game Preserve. As she watched the nasty sets of breakers explode on the beach, she couldn't help but think of her worst day ever on the water, on her New Zealand trip. In the morning it had taken her two hours to launch; she had capsized violently on five tries and sustained significant damage to her boat. She finally got out and paddled seven hours, but when she needed to land, the conditions were no better. On her approach to shore a hissing wall of water knocked her over, spun her around like a sock in a washing machine, and ripped the paddle from her hands (would-be kayakers, take note—this is why we bring a spare). Freya took it personally. "It was like the sea was laughing at me," she wrote at the time.

I've never been entirely convinced that what doesn't kill you makes you stronger, but it seems to be true in Freya's case. Thinking about the New Zealand fiasco didn't intimidate her; it made her more determined. She donned her helmet and waited and watched as the rollers rumbled by. When the last wave in a set passed, she took a deep breath and sprinted in just behind it like a rabid dog chasing the paper boy.

No big deal. She gave the episode one line in her blog: "I didn't even get a single drop in my face on landing," and then moved on to a more interesting topic—what to wear après swim, which is, obviously, "NO clothes, until you get chilly."

DAY 7: SATURDAY, JANUARY 24

Freya paddled just one hour before she was blown off the water by 30-knot winds. She spent one day sharing Woodside Beach with some families, fishermen, and 4x4s. When all was quiet, she cooked some dehydrated noodles—her staple dish—and turned in early. Rounding New Zealand's South Island, Freya came up with a "practical" solution to avoid the vicious sand flies that swarmed her whenever she crawled out of her tent at night. After dinner, which she cooked inside her tent, she brushed her teeth, spat the sudsy water into the crusty receptacle, and then pissed into the pot. She placed the tight-fitting lid on top of the funky mixture and went to sleep.

In the morning, she tossed the "nicely soaked, disinfected" contents into the ocean, rinsed the pot with salt water, and was good to go. "Who wants to scrub a dirty pot?" she said, proud of her solution. "Nobody."

I'm not normally squeamish, but this struck me as unsavory in the extreme. "Didn't it stink?" I asked.

"Never," she said, more amused still. "Never, never."*

And, yes, she used the same convenient system here in Australia.

DAY 8: SUNDAY, JANUARY 25

In her first week she had covered nearly 200 miles, more than she had paddled in the previous eight months. At the end of a 34-mile day, she passed a fisherman, waved hello, and headed ashore. Paradise Beach was deserted, so Freya stripped off her clothes and took her nightly swim.

---

* One of the main ingredients in urine is, in fact, ammonia, a disinfectant. Ammonia is also used to reduce the stinging and itching resulting from insect, jellyfish, and anemone encounters. Letterman fans might remember that Madonna once told Dave on his show that she used urine to cure athlete's foot fungus. And, during her days as a gymnast, Freya was told that urinating on her blisters would toughen her skin.

Tucked tight in her sleeping bag at 9:00, she heard a voice outside her tent. "Is anybody home?"

"Are you the lonely fisherman I passed?"

"Yes, that's me; I thought you might like some company."

"No thanks, I was already asleep."

"Would you like some coffee?" he asked.

"No, I'd like to sleep."

"I saw you having your nude swim. It looked lovely."

Polite but firm, she bid him adieu and unzipped her tent just far enough to hand him a postcard that featured the picture of her on tip-toes in a wet suit. He shuffled off and Freya surmised that he "probably had nice dreams on my lovely picture."

DAY 9: MONDAY, JANUARY 26

I can appreciate a good nude swim story as much as the next guy. And I fully sympathize with lone female travelers who have to deal with unwanted advances or worse from sexist dirt-bags. This fisherman did not seem to rate that designation, but maybe that was only because Freya had handled him so adroitly.* And yet when I read the story on her blog I mostly found myself irritated by another reference to her birthday suit— the seventh in nine days. Couldn't she tell us a little more about the landscape and culture that surrounded her? I had stopped looking for emotional revelations. Given how she felt about negative thinking, it wasn't so surprising that she had not offered a single word of complaint about the hardships or the danger. To Freya's way of thinking, to call something difficult would be to admit she was having difficulty, and that she would not do.

So if she wasn't going to pump up the adventure jam, couldn't she throw us a few sociological bones? She might have mentioned that the Brataualung clan of the Gunai people had been fishing the inlets in these parts in their dugout canoes for the better part of six thousand years

---

* She had remarkably few problems of this sort while in Australia. Although one morning she woke at first light and there, outside her tent waiting patiently, were three white-haired gents who had been following her trip online and wanted to say hello.

before Matthew Flinders and George Bass arrived in 1798 and began slaughtering seals and generally ruining the neighborhood. Or how about a good shark, snake, or stingray story? She had just passed Snake Island. Of the ten most poisonous snakes in the world, all are Australian. The inland taipan, the deadliest of all, produces enough venom in a single bite to kill a quarter-million mice. (To borrow Bill Bryson's line, the taipan "has a lunge so swift and a venom so potent that your last mortal utterance is likely to be: "I say, is that a sn—".)

But, to be fair, Freya was paddling from dawn to dusk without getting out of her boat. Launching and landing are where kayakers run the greatest risk of damage to their boat or their persons, and she chose lowering her risk profile—and covering more distance—over the possibility of meeting an interesting human or reptile. In her blog she wrote: "It happens that the most lovely beach is getting boring to look at as there is nothing happening ashore: no fishing lines to take care of, no bathing families to wave at, no marine mammals. Just the endless waves coming ashore which were still entertaining to watch and even ride on as I saw how close I could get without being caught and thrown sideways on the beach. Funny game."

Well, thank goodness for the Internet. I Googled Snake Island and learned, to my prurient delight, that the locals long ago used it as a nuptial island for newlywed couples.

Day 10: Tuesday, January 27

Two hundred and sixty-seven miles into her journey, Freya took her first rest day. Of course, rest is a relative term when we're talking about a woman who does thirty-two-thousand-piece jigsaw puzzles to relax. Hosted in Lake Entrance by a couple with two dachshunds, she woke early, washed her clothes, made minor gear repairs, weeded out surplus stuff, answered 163 e-mails, contacted several sponsors, shopped, and finally got her mobile Internet in order so on the days she had cell phone reception she would be able to blog, Skype, and check e-mail in the comfort of her own tent.

Total miles: 0; Total hours of sleep: 4

Day 11: Wednesday, January 28

Freya pulled up to a deserted beach at dusk. Something caught her eye, glistening at the water's edge—it was huge, shiny, and black. What in the name of Jacques Cousteau was it? First guess: a wide, flat rock. But why would it be sitting in the middle of an endless stretch of sand? Second guess: a giant turtle? A downed UFO?

She approached it like a hunter would a wounded animal. The thing was nearly 7 feet long and 5 feet wide and about as thick and flat as the *Encyclopedia Britannica*. And it had fins.

As she later learned from a fisherman, it was an ocean sunfish (*mola mola*)—a solid entrant for the strangest fish in the sea contest. These gentle giants, often mistaken for sharks because of their large dorsal fin, are the world's largest bony fish. While their average weight is around one ton, the biggest *mola* ever recorded was a 10-footer that tipped the scales at 4,927 pounds.

When Freya emerged from her tent in the morning, the giant fish that was in fact only average size was gone with the tide.

Day 12: Thursday, January 29

For the first time in nearly two weeks, Freya stopped for lunch. The swell was down and the inviting beach at Pearl Point offered an easy landing, and she had a hankering for something more substantial than her usual onboard lunch of crackers, dried fruit, cereal bars, and cheese sticks. There was a pre-cooked meal of couscous in the back hatch, but she couldn't get at it without landing, so she treated herself to sixty minutes on dry land.

She wasn't stopping because she was stiff and needed to stretch her legs. You can comb through Freya's blog and not find a single complaint about what sitting in a slim kayak for twelve hours a day does to your body. For the non-kayakers reading this, let me explain what this would be like for a normal person—me, for example. Three hours in a kayak is uncomfortable; double that and it's like flying coach in the middle seat with linebackers on either side and a nose guard sitting in front of you with his seat all the way back; double that time, and you had better be a former gymnast with the ass of a draft horse and a lower back like Gumby's.

Whenever she felt the need and the seas cooperated, Freya would lie back on the deck on her PFD*, which was almost always strapped on the boat behind her. She would raise her paddle over her head to stretch her chest muscles and relax her forearms by bending her hands back and forth. If the water was calm, she would take her legs out of the cockpit and dangle her dogs in the sea, or rest them on the deck like a football fan settling into a Barcalounger before the big game.

And that's pretty much the secret to Freya's incredible staying power in the boat. That and a gel seat cushion.

DAY 13: FRIDAY, JANUARY 30

Hoping to make plenty of hay in the morning before the headwinds arrived, Freya hit the water by six. In the early afternoon she stopped at the broad rocky headland to take a picture of the towering 130-foot lighthouse at Point Hicks. When Captain James Cook was approaching the Australian mainland in 1770, this was the point that inspired Lieutenant Zachary Hickes to shout the first *"Land ho!"* And though Cook was gracious enough to name it after him, he unfortunately screwed up the spelling. The historical record is vague as to whether dropping the "e" would eventually cost Hickes chicks back home. *No, wait, yes, it is Hickes with an "e" but I really was the first bloke to see Australia . . . !*

As she rounded Rame Head alongside Croajingolong National Park, the wind grew stronger and the sea turned wild. Freya enjoyed it. "Fun to paddle," she wrote in her blog. "My boat feels stable and secure in the rough stuff and at least falling asleep was not an option. But"—and this line made me scratch my head—"I was still paddling with closed eyes, as feeling the wind on my face makes it easy to keep direction."

When she opened her eyes and looked left into the bay behind Rame Head there were scores of seals, a school of dolphins, and an ominous fin she preferred not to identify.

Protected from the worst of the wind by the headlands, she counted down the kilometers from one to the next like a bored kid in the

---

* Personal flotation device, aka "life jacket."

backseat singing "A Hundred Bottles of Beer on the Wall." She could have pulled onto one of the beaches along the rocky coastline, but the forecast called for even stronger headwinds the next day. If she made it to the town of Mallacoota, she would be able to take a rest day with access to amenities.

But by 9:00 the sun had sunk below the horizon and the wind, which was blowing 20–25 mph, showed no signs of relenting. Although she was making woefully slow progress, once darkness fell she had no choice but to push on to Mallacoota, where she knew she could land. She turned on her SPOT messenger—a personal tracking device that works off satellites—to indicate that she was still out on the water, and carried on. "I kind of like the challenge of fighting headwinds," she wrote afterwards. "I needed some practice in night paddling anyway."

Around Bastion Head she saw two red lights. In Caffyn's description of this stretch of the coast, which she had read the night before, he mentioned a pair of red lights leading to a boat ramp just before the entrance to the inlet at Mallacoota. Although he had written about them twenty-seven years earlier, Freya bet on them being the same lights she now saw to her left. Straining to make out some sign of a beach in the inky darkness, she headed toward what sounded like an easy shallow landing.

Eighteen hours after climbing into her kayak, she stepped onto terra firma at last and dragged the boat away from the water. She stripped off her cold, wet clothes and went for a swim. As her tired muscles started to relax in the warm water, a male voice spoke.

"Midnight paddle, eh?" A flashlight shone in her eyes.

She nodded, too weary to talk. She waited for him to leave, covered her dripping torso with a sarong, and made her way through the dark to her boat, her tent, and a long, deep sleep.

DAY 14: SATURDAY, JANUARY 31

Freya finally posted a photo of her rash. And, yup, it was a doozy. "Keeping my skin healthy may be my biggest personal challenge on this trip," she wrote. "No sunburn problems, but this looks like a teenager in puberty. I got tea tree oil and some PawPaw ointment . . . we'll see."

Dozens of people wrote in with helpful suggestions, including someone named Hillary the herbalist. But the comment that grabbed my attention the most was the one written by an old Aussie kayaker: "You should have seen Andrew McAuley's back after his five-day Gulf crossing. He was on antibiotics for a week."

DAY 15: SUNDAY, FEBRUARY 1

Keeping Australia on her left, Freya crossed the border between Victoria and New South Wales, two of Australia's six states, and headed north along Nadgee National Park. She saw her first sharks off of Green Cape. How did she feel about that? As long as they weren't great whites—and these were not—it was OK by her.

In fact, she welcomed all encounters with marine life—she liked the company. That day she also met up with a school of "pleasant high-jumping black and white dolphins" and passed scores of seals basking in the sun belly up in the water, like my Grandma Hattie on her daily swim in Miami Beach.

The humans were another story. A sailboat crossed in front of her but either the sailors didn't see her or "they were too arrogant to wave at a simple kayaker."

Nothing like some righteous indignation over a real or imagined snub to get a paddler to pick up the pace.

DAY 17: TUESDAY, FEBRUARY 3

Camping near Tathra, Freya heard something scratching around outside her tent. When she couldn't ignore it any longer, she peeked out. There stood the world's largest marsupial, the one the aboriginals call *gangurru*.

DAY 18: WEDNESDAY, FEBRUARY 4

Being a professional adventurer isn't a day at the beach, even when you're actually on the beach. At least not if you're Freya Hoffmeister.

Take Day 18.

She woke at five. She was on the water from six in the morning to seven-thirty at night. She showered, set up camp, ate dinner, and then pecked away at her Toshiba Protégé R500-Y11 laptop until eleven.

"I worked online again too much!" she wrote that night. "It's a curse of carrying your own laptop." And of Australia's surprisingly consistent Internet access, Freya estimated that she had a connection 50 percent of the time, even in remote areas.

It seemed to me that skipping a night of blogging would be easy enough to justify. But that's not Freya's way. "The pressure I put on myself about updating my blog in a decent style piles up if I haven't been online for a while ... I can't say those hours off are relaxing mentally. My mind relaxes mostly on the water and my body on shore. I'd love to have both again at some point."

Three days later she was weather-bound in Burrill Beach. It was 104 degrees. To escape the heat, Freya wandered into a cafe in town. She devoured a stack of walnut banana pancakes and would have happily stayed put and worked online all afternoon, soaking up the AC, but the Internet connection stunk.

Back at the sweltering campground she found a crystal clear connection that was, oddly enough, just outside the entrance of the men's room. "It definitely was a good conversation starter," she said.

DAY 19: THURSDAY, FEBRUARY 5

In the afternoon Freya ran into a kayaker "of the other kind"—one, that is, with a small sail mounted on his deck.

Now, at this point you will be thinking either, "My god!" or "So?" There are those who believe a kayak is a kayak and a sailboat is a sailboat and never the twain should meet, and those who ascribe to more of a "whatever gets you down the road" philosophy. Caffyn was a kayak purist—no sail. Eric Stiller, on the other hand, begins his book about his attempted circumnavigation with the words "Tony! Let's set the sails!"—which should give you an idea of where he stood on the issue. While Eric and Tony Brown, his paddling partner, did debate the question before starting out, they broke out the sails on Day 3 of their expedition and never looked back. There were days when they barely took a stroke.

Eric and Tony's trip was plenty arduous, sails or no sails. But it wasn't strictly a human-powered trip, and isn't that the point of a kayak expedition? Freya made it clear where she stood in her blog entry that night. "I was not envious at all!" she wrote. "I will not use a sail at any point. I'm a paddler, not a sailor. My wide shoulders need to be a sail enough."

And so the passing kayak-sailor zipped off downwind and Freya continued bashing north toward Sydney—both of them convinced that they were doing the right thing.

DAY 20: FRIDAY, FEBRUARY 6

Paddling out from her overnight camp on Broullee Island, a pristine forty-two-acre nature reserve connected to the mainland by a sandbar, Freya found the Tasman Sea hot, flat, and boring. Without a headwind to offer a challenge, she found it hard to stay focused. Letting the boat drift, she fiddled with her gear for a while and then lounged topless to expose her skin sores to the sun's healing rays.

When she deemed it was time to get serious, she sat up, opting to remain topless. She dipped a thick sponge in the water and balanced it, dripping, on her head. She had also clipped clothespins on her earlobes to ward off seasickness.

One of the pleasures of paddling alone in a vast sea—you can look like a hung-over member of the *Sex Pistols* and only the seagulls will know.

DAYS 22–26: FEBRUARY 8–12

The wind had picked up and shifted to the south, right behind her. While a tailwind might sound like a godsend—to a surf ski paddler it would be—Freya found a big following sea physically and mentally draining. Her boat was so heavy that she couldn't catch and surf the waves. Instead, waves she never saw coming were constantly lifting her boat and passing uselessly underneath, making it hard to relax or eat.

She took a day off in Ulladulla, battled for another two days, and then benched herself again in a lifesaving club in Bulli (pronounced *bool-eye*, once the home of Aboriginals who called themselves the Wodi Wodi). Never mind how *she* felt, I personally was frustrated by the delay. Truth be told, three weeks into her journey I was checking her blog with the regularity of a night watchman at a Swiss clock factory. Right after I logged on in the morning, I checked to see how far she had gotten while I had been asleep. In the late afternoon I caught up on bloggers' comments, and I looked again before I turned off my computer in the evening, just in case. No matter how thin the storytelling or how lacking in local color, Freya's smile-laden posts piqued my interest on a variety of levels. On the ghoulish level, I had heard so many Aussies insisting she was destined to die that I signed on each day prepared for news of her grisly demise.

And even if I could let it go for a day, the Big O could not. Oscar called me on Skype each morning to discuss her progress. When I say discuss, I really mean he called to vent about the various ways in which she was stuffing it up. She was carrying too much equipment; she had no idea how to launch through surf; she had a weak stomach and how dare she blame her nausea on the sports nutrition drink he recommended. But all of these were quibbles in comparison to the diatribe he launched when she took her first day off in Ulladulla.

"Glicker!" he nearly shouted at me, his voice equal parts anger and disbelief. "It's blowing 35 knots up her bum. She could cover 20 km a day without taking a stroke! She—is—clueless!"

Forced to defend Freya, I reminded him that her success depended not on speed but on endurance. And that she was a sea kayaker, not a ski paddler. But that was wasted on Oscar, who was convinced he could do the trip not in half the time, but in a quarter of the time.

Oscar and Freya had had their differences, and I knew he resented that she had not listened to a word of the advice he had offered her in Hawaii. But more than that, he was—both of us were, in fact—more than a little jealous that she was the one having a go around a coastline that was as gorgeous and pristine as it was challenging and dangerous. Freya may have been high on hubris and low on speed, but facts were facts: Paddling nearly twelve hours a day for most of a month, this forty-four-year-old woman who had not trained in months had already taken 700 miles off her circumnavigation to-do list. And made it look easy.

Day 27: Friday, February 13

On Friday morning Freya checked the weather forecast from Karel. It called for 10–15 knots before noon, increasing to 20 knots and seas of

7–10 feet in the afternoon—heads-up conditions, but technically within the reach of anyone confident of paddling around Australia.

From Bulli to Manly Beach in Sydney is 50 miles. Tony King had spoken to Freya about a press event they had arranged for Friday evening—interviews with a TV station and two daily newspapers. With a big following sea, Freya thought she could make it in time. Tony and Jacqui, his wife and business partner, felt that Sydney presented the best opportunity to publicize the trip and had spent considerable time coordinating this event, which was meant to be the start of a national media campaign with local newspapers, radio stations, and news channels organized to cover Freya's trip and interview her along the east coast of Australia.

While Tony is as mellow as merino wool, Jacqui is a fiery sort. She and Freya had not hit it off when they'd met in Oahu eight months earlier, and it hadn't helped matters that the Kings had rushed off on their Christmas holiday the day Freya first arrived, leaving her to cool her heels in town for three extra days waiting for her boat to be readied. Jacqui also had serious concerns about Epic's sponsoring someone she perceived to be at best ill-equipped to succeed and at worst delusional. Andrew McAuley's boat manufacturer had been sued after his death; what would it mean for Epic if Freya went down in their boat?

There is some disagreement about what transpired the day Freya was to paddle into Sydney. According to Jacqui, the plans were clear, and Freya simply didn't show and didn't have the courtesy to let them know. According to Freya, she knew she was expected on Friday, but she had never agreed to paddle into Sydney Harbor, which would have tacked on unnecessary miles.

And besides, she was busy.

Twenty miles south of Sydney, Freya headed north along a stretch of jagged, nearly unbroken sandstone cliffs. After three consecutive days of 30-knot winds out of the south, the ocean streaked forward as if it was littered with a million flying carpets cruising to Sydney. As the day wore on, the wind picked up; when she reached the cliffs the swell was 12–15 feet. That translates to waves with 24- to 30-foot faces, with the tops of the bigger ones breaking white. Even a mile off shore, the rebound off the cliffs collided with Mack truck–sized swells, tossing her around like a ping-pong ball in a lottery machine. She turned her bow into the breaking stuff and got a stiff neck from looking over her shoulder for trouble. It felt as if for every kilometer she traveled forward, she covered twice that vertically.

Eating was difficult at best. Holding an apple in one hand with her paddle, she would snatch bites between strokes. She ate two apples in seven hours, with a few sips of fresh water to rinse the salt from her mouth. Water seeped through the drum-tight neoprene spray skirt covering her cockpit and sloshed around her legs. Although she was wearing a long-sleeved polypro shirt under a long-sleeve jacket with a PFD on top, as the day wore on she became chilled through. Had she and the Kings been best mates she would still not have been able to make a phone call.

By 5:00 she had come just 24 miles. At the heads just south of Botany Bay, the famed spot where Captain Cook first landed in 1770, she had a decision to make: Push on to Manly, where reporters were on hold in various watering holes around the harbor, or head in. She didn't deliberate long. She turned left and paddled past the rock engravings at Jibbon Head, past the beach in Bundenna (an Aboriginal word meaning "noise like thunder") and finally stopped for the night in a park in Port Hacking, the Sydney suburb where the fourth season of *Australia's Next Top Model* was filmed.

Said Freya: "I felt a bit guilty, but there was no way my energy and concentration would last to my planned destination. I was sorry about the gathered crowd waiting for me there." Freya tried to call Tony, she said, but couldn't reach him. Tony had called her about twenty times that day, but she had not been answering her phone.

Jacqui King's e-mail to me at the time included the words "pathological narcissist" and "cow." (She may have also mentioned a certain favor that she would like to ask of a great white shark.) Jacqui wasn't buying that the conditions alone were responsible for Freya's no-show. She wrote: "Not sure how big it actually was; there was a reasonable swell coming in through the heads yesterday afternoon. Confirms in my mind that she has no idea what is ahead of her."

But it got worse. When Freya didn't show on Friday, the Kings asked the gathered media to return on Saturday morning. Freya wasn't even sure she could paddle in the morning, the seas were so big. "At best," Freya told me, "I'd have arrived late on Saturday." Later that night Tony read on Freya's blog that she planned to spend Saturday on shore. He and Jacqui quickly contacted the reporters with more apologies and put them on hold until they could find out from Freya exactly when she would be where. They repeatedly tried to reach Freya, by phone and e-mail, but heard nothing from her—until Saturday night, when she called from a cold, rainy, deserted Shelley Beach in Sydney to let them know she had arrived. Tony told her that if she could stay in Sydney on Sunday and leave Monday morning, they would rally the media again and arrange for a flotilla of kayakers to accompany her out of the harbor. He tried to call her many times on Sunday, but the first they heard from her was an e-mail at 7:00 that night. Freya was in Terrigal—an hour north of Sydney.

As far as Tony and Jacqui were concerned, Epic had missed out on a valuable PR opportunity and they had lost credibility with important media contacts. As far as Freya was concerned, the Kings "didn't give a shit about the trip. The whole vibe with them was horrible."

She dealt with the mess Freya-style—she moved on.

CHAPTER FIVE

Water Nymphs Online

Have you ever noticed that anybody driving slower than you is an idiot, and anyone going faster than you a maniac?

—GEORGE CARLIN

IN EARLY MARCH, AS FREYA WAS MOVING UP THE GOLD COAST, I FLEW to Australia to attend the Surf Lifesaving Championships in Perth and interview a bunch of surf ski paddlers for a book I was thinking about writing. It was my first time in the country, but having looked at the map of Australia on Freya's blog every day for the last month to keep tabs on her position, I was pretty solid on my Aussie geography. The right side of the continent looks like a buffalo's head in profile: Melbourne is at the mouth, Brisbane at the bulging forehead, Mackay at the top of the bowed head, and Cape York at the tip of the elongated horn, practically poking the underbelly of Papua New Guinea. Freya had organized her trip into fifteen stages. She had completed Stage One, Melbourne to Sydney, on Day 28, and Stage Two on Day 44, when she pulled into Brisbane.

While I had the map down, my grasp on all other things Australian was as tenuous as Mel Gibson's standing with the Anti-Defamation League. Of course I knew that the first blokes to arrive on these "fatal shores"* were convicts from Mother England. (That "First Fleet," as it came to be known, arrived in 1788 with 750 petty criminals. It seemed like such a good solution to prison overcrowding that they sent another

---

* *The Fatal Shore: The Epic of Australia's Founding* by Robert Hughes is the definitive history of England's decision to send its convicts to Australia.

165,000 prisoners over the next eighty years.) But what else did I know? As a kid I'd had a boomerang and in adult life I'd banged boats with enough Aussies to know not to say "shrimp on the barbie"—*prawns* is the preferred term—and to call a big wave that breaks outside the surf zone a "bombie." Although I only recently learned that the word is derived from the Aboriginal *bomborra*. I had assumed it was the diminutive of "bomb," which is how I experienced these aquatic explosions.

Recognizing that there were cavernous gaps in my knowledge about the world's biggest island, I spent the first six hours of my twenty-two-hour flight reading *Breath*, a novel by Tim Winton about three extreme surfers in Western Australia. I was struck (and not in a good way) by this description of the mountainous swell in the Indian Ocean, where I would soon be paddling: "On TV I'd seen elephants run beside safari jeeps, pounding along at incredible speed while seeming to move in slow motion, and that's exactly how it was."

I took a nap, watched four episodes of *Flight of the Conchords*, and then cracked *In a Sunburned Country* by Bill Bryson. Though he's a huge fan of Australia, he admits "only Antarctica is more hostile to life." Not only is Australia "wondrously venomous and toothy," according to Bryson it is "a country where even the fluffiest caterpillars can lay you out with a toxic nip, where seashells will not just sting you but actually sometimes go for you."

So, assuming Freya survived the swells and the three 100-mile stretches of cliffs that stood in her way, the great whites and the saltwater crocs, she would also have to avoid five lethal critters I had never even heard of: the funnel web spider, box jellyfish, blue-ringed octopus, paralysis tick, and stonefish—all of which produce the kind of fiendish serum Dr. No could have used to achieve world domination. Freya's steady progress up the coast had almost convinced me she could pull off this trip; by the time I landed, I put her chances at fifty-fifty at best.

And now I was back among the very Australian paddlers who had predicted the worst right from the beginning. Yes, they were largely a sexist and jingoistic bunch, but after paddling in their home waters I could see they also had a point. On my third day in Sydney, I went for a 10-mile downwind paddle with two locals. We were at least a mile from shore when I felt a burning sensation on my right forearm. *How the hell did I get tangled in a fishing line so far from shore?* I wondered . . . until the translucent line slid down the sleeve of my rash guard and onto the bare skin on the back of my hand.

"Fuckin' jellies!" I shouted, flinging the gelatinous goop into the sea.

To my right, Karl Treacher, a former pro triathlete who had taken up paddling a few years back, was smirking like a jack-o'-lantern. "Welcome to the bluebottle club, mate! Care for me to piss on it?"

"It feels as if my arm is on fire," I complained an octave above my normal macho pitch.

"Wait 'til the pain spreads to your balls!"

"Pretty funny," I replied.

"Not joking," he said, laughing harder.

By the time we had shouldered our skis up the steep hill to his car, the pain had spread to my abdomen and my jewels felt as if they had been lathered in liniment. Apparently the local swimmers, surfers, and paddlers are stung so often that they build immunity to the poison—except not always. In 2006, Karl and a friend named Wes were training for Molokai. They paddled out of Sydney Harbor, past North Head, straight into a patch of bluebottles. Wes, a Navy commando trained to suffer, flicked a "big bastard" onto his broad back with his paddle and recoiled as if he had been electrocuted. He fell off his ski into a mess of bluebottles and by the time he had wiggled out of the tentacles wrapped around his neck his ski had blown away. Karl had him flop on to the back of his ski and, struggling to shore, flipped more bluebottles on them both. When they finally reached land, Wes was in respiratory shock. "I took him to hospital," said Karl, "and then went home and screamed in the shower for two hours as all the glands in my body swelled—including my nuts, which grew to the size of baseballs. We both sported scars for the best part of a year."

Freya had been stung by bluebottles on Day 23, but had given it such short shrift on her blog that when I read it in my slippers back home I figured it was no big whoop. To quote her exactly: "First bluebottle wrap, but OK."

I asked her afterwards whether it hurt. "Hurt like hell," she said. "Right," I said, opting not to mention my testicles.

During the three weeks I paddled in Australia, it seemed that I got my ass kicked every other day. On two separate occasions I bent my rudder and lost my sunglasses in the shore break; on the Gold Coast I took a wave to the left side of my face that knocked a contact lens out of my eye and left me with a sore neck for a week. In Mooloolaba on the Sunshine Coast, I fought back panic heading out into double head-high surf and, on the way back, got dragged by a wave and broke a foot strap. I wondered at what point my mates would stop letting me borrow their boats.

Then there were the big fish stories. Paddling with two friends just north of Sydney, I hung my legs over the side of my ski when we stopped to regroup, only to be told, "If you value your feet, put 'em back in the boat, mate!" Gallows humor Aussie style, I thought, until I got an earful about the great white that patrolled the area, preying on humpback babies passing by on their annual migration. For the next five minutes it was scare-the-shit-out-of-the-Yank time: Last year a white pointer, or great white shark, had flipped a kayak fisherman into the drink at Long Reef and circled him for a full minute before moving on. Last week a bull shark had attacked a diver in Sydney harbor, swiping a hand and leg.

As if to drive home the message, the next morning the *Sydney Morning Herald* had a story about a great white that attacked a surfer off the southern end of Bondi Beach, just a few miles south of where I was sipping a mocha latte in Manly. Where I paddled back home in Brooklyn, my biggest concerns (aside from keeping well away from mobster John Gotti's yacht, *Not Guilty*) were drunken power boaters and aggressive swans. Paddling in Oz I often felt like an extra in *Jaws* with Robert Shaw nowhere to be found.

Not Freya. Passing Sydney two weeks earlier, she spotted "two lovely fins" circling her kayak. These fins happened to belong to hammerheads, not great whites, and although they can reach 20 feet long and weigh five thousand pounds, they rarely dine on humans. Still, there aren't that many paddlers I know who refer to these mallet-headed, sci-fi-ugly predators as "lovely." Going by the statistics, though, Freya had the right attitude toward the beasts. There had been just twenty shark attacks in all of Australia in 2009, which meant she was more likely to be killed by bees than a shark. But she was paddling a friggin' sea kayak around Australia—that had to skew the odds a little, didn't it? Paddling up along the Great Barrier Reef, she felt something slam the back of her boat. What? She didn't know. All she said about the incident was that her boat wasn't damaged and it made her think of what she would do "just in case." To another out-of-towner paddling in the same waters at the same time, fretting over imaginary fins and dark shadows underwater—that is, whenever I wasn't busy breaking my boat in the crashing surf—her lack of paranoia was hard to believe. By the time my three weeks in Australia were up and I was heading home, I was impressed by the way Freya had handled the east coast. On the other hand, everyone I spoke with said this was the "easiest" water she would encounter.

On Saturday, March 7, Freya made it to Hervey Bay—seven weeks and 1,379 miles into her journey. Weary from eighteen continuous days of paddling and longing to give her sore skin a chance to heal, she decided to take a day off on Sunday and return to the water on Monday. However, on Sunday morning the weather service reported that Cyclone Hamish, which had formed up around Cape York, had intensified to a Category 5 storm with 130 mph winds and was heading south. That evening a thousand people were evacuated from Fraser Island, the 75-mile-long by 15-mile-wide sand island that shelters Hervey Bay. By Monday, the normally flat Great Sandy Strait was a seething muddy mess; by Tuesday branches were flying around town. The tide had come up nearly 20 feet and flooded the harbor. The beaches were gone. Sitting out the storm in the cozy home of Janita and David Knowles, Freya wrote on her blog, "I wonder if my tent would have survived on a beach somewhere out on the Great Barrier Reef. . . .TV pictures show conditions further north that you just wouldn't want to be in."

Twenty-seven years earlier—April 7, 1982—Paul Caffyn was 1,100 miles north of Hervey Bay in the Coral Sea, squinting through grey, overcast skies growing darker by the minute. He was a dozen miles off the coast of Cape Melville, island-hopping along the Great Barrier Reef. Finally the low profile of Stainer Islet came into focus and he breathed a sigh of relief. The wind had whipped the sea white and rain was falling in sheets by the time he pulled his kayak up on the one-acre island of sand and scrub. Once inside his tent he listened to the wind intensify. To his horror, the radio reported that Cyclone Dominic, formed over the Gulf of Carpentaria, was heading his way. The high point on Stainer was 3 feet above the high-water mark. If he stayed put, the storm surge could deliver him to oblivion. Twice he packed up to head out to the much larger Burkitt Island 6 miles west, but changed his mind each time after he put the boat in the water.

In the morning, much of the beach was covered in water—an ominous sign, as high tide was still three hours away. Caffyn moved his camp to the center of the island and secured everything to the lone tree, a stunted casuarina. Waves broke over his old campsite. He was in the middle of Pelican Island Reef, population zero, with no real way of communicating with anyone. He had a walkie-talkie, but he was well out of range of his support crew. To keep the mounting terror at bay, he read and re-read an old *Reader's Digest* (a fate nearly as bad as being swept away by a cyclone). Finally, the storm veered off shore after two sleepless nights, and he made a dash to Cape Sidmouth. Camped under a full moon, he built a fire of driftwood, cooked the last of his dehydrated food and, serenaded by frogs, gave thanks. "The relief of being alive was just so enormous. . . ."

—⁓—

Luck is the X-factor in any trip of this magnitude. Caffyn had been in the wrong place at the wrong time when his cyclone hit. Freya was luckier, although she didn't see it that way. She was pinned down by Hamish in Hervey Bay for five days, four more than she wanted. "I'm like a race horse," she wrote, "I would rather want to gooooooooooooooooooo!!!!!!!!!!!!!"

During her forced rest, Freya got caught up on her blog and her faithful bloggers got caught up with her. Describing her raw lower back and the sores under her arms ("I reckon I have to put on a shirt again to paddle," she wrote), she got plenty of skin care tips, ranging from the liberal application of anhydrous lanolin (a waxy substance secreted by sheep that I once used to break in my baseball gloves) to a back massage, which a blogger from a small town in the United States generously offered to administer. Freya sought tech support for her ailing Olympus Stylus 1030 camera. She also received a lot of unsolicited advice on the best way to avoid the crocodiles patrolling the coastal waters from Cairns to Cape York.

"Hire a support boat," suggested a blogger from Germany. "Carry a rifle," wrote a local from Queensland, "because crocs love kayaks and will regularly charge and you'll need to defend yourself from attack." Someone else simply posted a story from the *Daily Telegraph* from 2007 about a rancher in north Queensland who took a bad fall from his horse and wandered into a marshland that, he quickly realized, was crawling with crocs. He scrambled up a tree with nothing more than the clothes on his back and two ham sandwiches in his pocket. For six days and nights, two sets of red eyes stared unblinkingly up at him while he desperately fought off sleep. On day seven he was spotted by an army helicopter and winched to safety.

If such stories bothered her, she didn't say. And then she made the announcement that silenced all talk of crocs. Crocs were dangerous animals, no question, but again the statistics were in her favor. For what Freya was planning now, there were no statistics. After rounding the tip of Cape York, she said, she would do an open-ocean crossing of the massive Gulf of Carpentaria rather than hug the coast, as Caffyn had. It would save her four weeks—if she survived.

——◆——

"She's fucked in the head!" Oscar declared the next morning.

For once I was in complete agreement with the big redhead. It was 330 miles straight across some famously turbulent water. On her trip so far, a really big day for Freya was 50 miles; in the Gulf, assuming she had following seas, she would be out at least a week without touching land. And too far from shore to have much hope of rescue if things went wrong.

"After two days without sleep she'll be so buggered she won't know which direction to paddle," Oscar said.

"Is she really that confident?" I asked.

"No," he replied, "just that dense!"

Freya conceded that she would have to "pick the right weather window to have some more or less quiet water," and detailed a few sleeping options that revolved around using her paddles as pontoons to stabilize the boat at night. "I prefer a setup on top of the boat. I could stay seated with my legs inside the cockpit and lie comfortably on the back deck with my butt lifted on a pillow."

Better than sleeping in a stockade, I thought, *but hardly comfortable*.

The blog-readers leapt into action with a barrage of warnings and advice. An Aussie paddler who had recently been stalked by a 9-foot tiger shark told her to take a shark shield—a device that generates a protective electrical field. "I've not seen this number of sharks about in my 48 years," he wrote. A Hawaiian suggested she remove the bulkheads in her boat and slide her whole body inside to sleep, like Ed Gillet did in 1987 when he paddled and sailed his kayak from Monterey to Maui. A Dutchman suggested her best option for slumber would be a small inflatable raft. A German who had lived in the Philippines cautioned against using her paddles as outriggers. Bamboo or sewer pipe were better, he wrote, a reasonable suggestion that ended on an enigmatic note: "If you want to be a Cowboy, you have to think like an Indian."

Freya didn't respond to this flurry of posts. Instead she slept late and ate lots of homemade veggie pizza. She finally weighed everything in her kayak on a bathroom scale: boat, 55 lbs + gear, 83 lbs + food for 14 days, 55 lbs. + water for 5 days, 26 lbs = 219 lbs + paddler, 165 lbs = 384 lbs. She studied her maps for the next stage, to Mackay, and mailed two food parcels up the coast. The night before she left for Mackay, however, she read a post that she felt compelled to answer. Some poor sap had made the mistake of referring to her "attempt" to circle Australia. Writing in 20-point type, Freya snapped, "**I'm not attempting it.**"

She switched to even bigger type for the kicker: "**I'm doing it.**" Followed by, "Please correct. Thanks."

Before you could say *Edmund Hillary wasn't Sir until he succeeded in his attempt*, wordsmiths around the world were weighing in to support the original use of the transitive verb. In their view, a circumnavigation—a complete lap around a designated landmass—remains an "attempt" up until the moment it is "done." (Otherwise, my stroll up Manly beach could also be construed as a circumnavigation.) The wordsmiths were roundly countered by members of the "you-go-girl" camp: "Of course you're just doing it and of course you cannot look at it any other way!" And, "Don't worry about the semantics. You ARE doing it right now."

I sided with the wordsmiths, although my issue was more about hubris than usage. Still, when Oscar called the next morning, I complained, "The woman needs a dictionary."

"She's a flippin' nitwit," he concurred reliably.

Meanwhile, as Oscar and I Skyped our quibbles, Freya was somewhere between Toogoom and Agnes Water, paddling topless to a showdown with the Gulf.

———

For the next 416 miles and nine days Freya cruised north like she was on Ventura Boulevard with the top down. There were a few speed bumps, of course:

She stopped twice to fix a leak in the stern hatch.

She passed through a (live) military bombing range.

Camped above a steep harbor wall in Crowdy Head, she woke to find her boat missing. Luckily, an onshore wind had it pinned against the harbor wall. The next day she was rounding Point Plomer when a wave flipped her ass over teakettle—her first capsize of the trip. Said Freya: "It was my boat's revenge for me not taking care of it at Crowdy Head."

She saw two signs warning boaters about crocs and took extra care to find a safe campsite.

She bashed into the famed East Australian current, which—as you know if you've been coerced into watching *Finding Nemo* as many times as I have—is great if you're heading south to Sydney to rescue your son but a bitch if you're paddling north to Cape York. Freya fought her way through nasty chop off Cape Townshend; had her life jacket plucked off the back deck by a wave; and left her mobile phone on Wild Duck Island.

In short, another typical stretch of the Australian coast. She averaged 46.2 miles per day, despite taking time to test the sleeping system she aimed to use across the Gulf. She finished Stage 3 in Mackay on March 21, Day 63 of her . . . attempt. Hosted on a scheduled off day by a couple who lived in the rain forest, she made time for a boulder-hopping hike up the Pioneer River with two other women to a secluded natural pool beneath a waterfall. Did they swim? They did. Did they wear swimsuits? Of course not.

By the time they returned home, the "man of the house" had fiber-glassed her dinged hull and a neighbor had fixed the zipper on her tent. That gave Freya time to update her blog and post four—count 'em, four—color shots of the day's merriment. To my dismay, she used the term "water nymphs" twice.

Just so we're clear, I'm pro-nudity when there's water involved. But I get huffy when, for example, I'm trying to watch a Knicks game and a dozen women in itty-bitty sailor suits storm the court every time play stops. Is this the basketball game, or did I sit on the remote and switch to *Wild on Daytona Beach*? It's distracting, if not downright manipulative. And Freya's glamour shot, in which she posed on some rocks below the falls, her arm *just* hiding her breasts, her knee up *just* enough to hide her privates, was clearly staged for maximum distraction.

Freya often called updating her blog a chore, and I'm sure that's how it felt sometimes after twelve hours on the water. At the same time, for a woman with no female friends, who was currently (and frequently) between boyfriends, the one-sided dialogue with admiring paddlers from around the world was like salve for sore skin. How to keep everyone inter-ested and tuning in? In case it wasn't enough to paddle alone in huge seas teeming with lethal predators, on pace to set a record, she chose to work the "sexiest woman in kayaking" angle as well. And like 3-inch heels or a Victoria's Secret bra, it was working like a charm. A blogger named John requested she post larger pictures. "You are paddling's most beauti-ful woman." A Turk named Ugur concurred, adding the adjectives, "Brave, restless, and strong." For Peter, though, the pictures posed a problem: "My wife won't let me read your posts anymore."

❦

On her first day out of Mackay, Freya was miles off shore when a bombie dropped on her head. The 2006 winner of the Greenland National Rolling Championships nailed the roll but lost another life jacket, which had been tucked under the netting on the back deck as usual. She crossed another firing range, watched butterflies mating miles off shore, and saw 6-foot sea snakes slithering across the sea's surface. She was now within the Great Barrier Reef, the largest living thing on Earth, which encompasses roughly nine hundred islands and stretches for sixteen hundred miles from Fraser Island in the south to Papua New Guinea in the north.

Over the next nine days, Freya stuck to her routine, banging out another 419 miles. Given the (mostly) flat water, she characterized the paddling conditions as "boring" and "uneventful." The crocodile conditions were something else again. She avoided the croc-ridden shallows by camping on pristine islands well out to sea, and so far the strategy was working—she reached Cairns on Day 74 without even a sighting. But from reading her blog, it was easy to tell that she had *Crocodylus porosus* on the brain: The word "croc" appears seven times, the word "topless" only once.

A tropical city of 120,000 people, Cairns was Freya's last point of resupply before two more weeks of island-hopping along the Great Barrier Reef to the top of Australia. Then, after 2,000 miles of pushing north, she would finally turn west—and run smack into the Gulf of Carpentaria. While the bloggers continued to debate the pros and cons (mostly cons) of Freya's proposed shortcut, it was clear she was more focused on the 540 miles of prime crocodile habitat that she would have to negotiate to get there. Of all the hazards inherent in her trip, this was the only one that seemed to faze her at all. Crocs were essentially a nonfactor for Paul Caffyn—back when he paddled these waters, salties had been hunted to the verge of extinction. In the early 1970s crocs were given protected status,

67

and by the time Freya started her trip they had bounced all the way back. Because, short of a gun, what can stop a crocodile? Let's look at the facts:

- An adult male crocodile can grow longer than an Epic kayak and weigh as much as seventeen hundred pounds more than boat, paddler, and gear combined.
- A crocodile's top speed on land varies based on its size, but in full flight, despite weighing more than a grand piano, these stubby-legged creatures can hit 11 mph. How fast is that? Put it this way: If you can run a mile in under five and a half minutes, which not too many people can do, you can—probably—outrun a croc.
- Crocodiles can live on one meal a year if necessary. During lean times they simply wait, using the sun's heat to regulate their body temperature. In other words, if you are treed by a croc, don't count on it slinking off to find food until after it no longer matters.
- Crocs are masters of the sneak attack. An 18-footer can conceal himself in a foot of muddy water. Some salties have learned to hide when they hear the sound of footsteps or a car parking—and not because they're scared, if you catch my drift.*

But maybe I've made it sound too one-sided. If a croc slams its trap on you, you can always try poking it in the eye. If that doesn't work, crocs have a sensitive flap in the throat called the glottis that they use for breathing, so option two is to force your arm down its throat to the glottis

---

* Consider the story told to me by a paddler named Dave Winkworth. He and two partners were twenty-nine days into a 1,500-mile trip along the Great Barrier Reef from Cairns to Thursday Island when they stopped on uninhabited Macarthur Island. Dave's mate Arunas Pilka waded out into the shallows. Suddenly Arunas let out "a half scream, half shout" and the surface around him began to froth and foam. Winkworth ran out in the thigh-deep water and saw that a big crocodile had Arunas by the leg and was trying to sweep him off his feet in a death-roll. Arunas jammed his fingers in the croc's nostrils and when that failed to release the viselike grip, he thrust his hands in the croc's mouth, cutting his hand on teeth. The 6 3″, 210-pound Winkworth leapt onto the croc's back, wrapped his arms around its smooth hard belly, and hung on like a rodeo cowboy until it suddenly let go and darted away with a flick of its tail. Arunas' right leg was a mass of punctures and ripped flesh. Dave and the third member of the group sent out a distress signal, and two anxious hours after the attack Arunas was flown off in a chopper to a hospital on Thursday Island.

to encourage it to release you. Just be sure to do it before the death roll begins, as that will likely break or sever your arm.

Because crocs patrol river mouths, mangroves, and estuaries along the coast, Freya's plan was simple: stay far off shore, working headland to headland, island to island. In effect, paddle where the crocs ain't. Because these perfect predators can swim dozens of miles from shore—one blogger mentioned that crocs have been known to commute from Cape York to Papua New Guinea—this was no guarantee of safety, but it did improve the odds. Crocodiles had turned back Sandy Robson, the one other female expedition paddler to have made it from Melbourne to Cairns, and Freya was determined not to suffer the same fate.

At the end of 2006, Sandy Robson took a leave from her job as the Outdoor Ed Coordinator at a girls' school in Perth to begin what she called S.L.A.P.—Sandy's Long Australian Paddle—a solo, unsupported adventure to see how far she could get around the continent in one year. She left Melbourne in December, twenty-five years to the day after Caffyn completed his unprecedented voyage.

Five months later, she arrived at Cape Sidmouth, the spot Caffyn landed after his tense two-day stay on Stainer Island. As Sandy approached the beach, she saw what she thought was a croc basking in the sun and decided to push on another 15 miles north to Night Island. Although the island was extremely "mangrovy"—in other words, croc-friendly—the sun was setting and she needed to stop. She dragged her kayak past the high-water mark with all the confidence of someone approaching a derelict house with the door slightly ajar. But she set up her tent near a frangipani bush, placed her boat in front to serve as a mini barricade, and felt relatively safe.

After dinner, she walked away from her tent for a bathroom break. Scanning the beach with her flashlight, a pair of devilish red eyes peered back at her. She raced back to camp, her heart in her mouth, and called a friend on her satellite phone who advised her to build a fire to deter the croc from coming closer at high tide. Robson could light a fire with wet toilet paper, but never had it seemed to take longer to bring a blaze to life.

As the flames rose the croc retreated to the security of the mangroves. She returned to the beach every hour to stoke the fire and each time the ugly bastard had crept closer, only retreating again when the flames stood tall.

At first light she packed her boat and slipped away like a cat burglar past a night watchman. She paddled to the coast at Cape Direction and after rounding the point spotted a sheltered beach with an ideal campsite. She was gliding through calm, murky water toward the shore when she heard what sounded like bricks crashing down on the back end of her kayak. Turning around, her worst fears were confirmed. A large croc had clamped down on the back of her kayak. It let go, but it was still just behind. Sandy had been advised that if she saw a croc in the water she should just paddle away—but which way?

I considered whether my situation would allow me to paddle out to sea, rather than be chased off the water and onto the shore. Bugger that! In order for me to paddle out of this bay and back out to sea I would have to face a big croc head on—not an option. I happily paddled as fast as I could away from gaping croc jaws and towards the beach. All I could think was "Please don't get me, Please don't get me, Please don't get me, Please don't get me . . ." all the way to the beach. Actually I don't think I just thought it, I said it out loud like some kind of mantra. I did not know if I would be able to pull my spray deck loop, leap out and run up the beach fast enough. This is the place where I knew I would be the most vulnerable to an attack. I took a glance behind to see if I had a croc on my tail. Shit where is it? The bow of the kayak hit the sand and I already had the spray deck off and was running up the beach, thankfully without getting tangled up in my paddle leash. No croc chased behind me so I was able to relax a little and hurriedly pull my kayak up out of the danger zone. Then I saw it in the bay arching its back, puffing itself up and fully displaying its tail. This had certainly been a territorial attack from a large male croc.

Long, nightmarish ordeal made short, she portaged her gear and kayak to the other side of the point, set up camp, and called the local friend of a friend, who appeared the next morning in a small motorboat and brought her back to his rustic home. She spent a week there, thinking things over. But Robson knew that the next thousand miles of coast had even more crocs, and she had heard, firsthand, the story of a close encounter with a croc just a bit farther north from an experienced paddler from New South Wales.

She packed up and headed home, leaving the door open for some other female paddler to become the first to circumnavigate Australia— assuming she could get past the crocs.

Freya made it to Stainer Island a week after she left Cairns. She paid her respects to the lone casuarina tree to which Caffyn had secured himself as Cyclone Dominic raged near. The following afternoon, she skirted Night Island. And two days later, Day 87 of her trip, she landed on Restoration Island.

When she pulled her boat up the soft white sand beach, David Glasheen, a bare-chested, bushy-bearded, sixty-seven-year-old Sydney transplant who lives alone on the island with his brown mutt Quasi, greeted her with a broad smile and glass of white wine. By his side was another guest, a young French woman named Pasquale. After ten days of avoiding crocs on remote islands along the Great Barrier Reef, it was a relief to experience civilization again, such as it was.

Restoration Island played a part in one of the most famous sea stories of all time—the subject of countless books, four major films (starring, in order, Errol Flynn, Clark Gable, Marlon Brando, and Mel Gibson) and an episode of *The Simpsons*. The famed mutiny on the Bounty began on April 28, 1789, when master's mate Fletcher Christian, more than a tad cross at having to leave the topless beauties of Tahiti (one in particular), turned against his captain, William Bligh, and set him and eighteen of his loyal men adrift in a 23-foot open launch and high-tailed it back to Tahiti. On the first island they reached, one of Bligh's crew members was stoned to death by natives; four days later, sailing past Fiji, they were chased by hostile cannibals in canoes. Navigating without charts and with only minimal provisions, they endured huge seas that forced them to bail around the clock. Finally, after twenty-six days at sea, the half-dead crew landed on the sandy shores of a one-hundred-acre oasis that Bligh dubbed Restoration Island. (Not only were they literally "restored," it was the anniversary of the Day of Restoration of King Charles II.) Bligh used the mirror from his sextant to start a fire and the men ate a hearty stew of rock oysters, birds, and fish. After three days of easy living, they shoved off on a forty-seven-day, 3,600-mile trip to Timor in the Dutch West Indies, one of the greatest small-boat voyages in maritime history. Remarkably, nearly all of them made it safely back England, two years after they had first set sail. Some of those who had mutinied were tracked down and dealt with; Fletcher Christian (who married a Tahitian princess) eluded capture by the British but was eventually killed by Tahitians.

With a shoulder-length shaggy white mane and matching beard, Glasheen looked like a cross between Charlton Heston's Moses and Santa Claus as he showed Freya around his idyllic digs. Largely self-sufficient, Glasheen eats fish and native plants like lemongrass and capers, and raises bok choy, tomatoes, and corn, sometimes with the help of volunteers who work for a month or so in return for food and lodging. He brews beer and trades it for prawns from trawlers that stop by. He used a turbine to generate electricity until it was disabled in a storm; now he has a solar panel to power his computer and lights.

Under a canopy of stars, Dave grilled fish for his guests in an open barbecue pit. Afterwards, while Dave drank his homemade brew, Pasquale gave Freya a massage with lavender oil. "That's island life!" Freya wrote the next day, which she spent lounging around and updating her blog (incredibly, Dave has Internet access). She posted photographs of Dave showing off his succulent fruit trees, Dave with a glass of wine in hand, Dave flipping fillets on the barbie (sorry, Australian people), all with the self-satisfied smile of someone who had escaped the rat race for true peace and prosperity. Even his dog Quasi seemed smug.

Freya had contacted him in advance to arrange her stay and must have known something about him, but she didn't feel the need to profile him for her readers. I was intrigued by the idea of a modern-day Robinson Crusoe and thought there might be a good story there. It turned out there was a great story, and many journalists had already covered it. Glasheen was a business executive from Sydney who lost ten million bucks in the stock market crash of 1987; his marriage, which had produced two daughters, ended roughly the same time. In the early 1990s he paid a hefty sum for a fifty-year lease on one-third of the island (the rest is a national park) and moved there with his girlfriend. While romantic in theory, island life proved too rustic for the girlfriend and after just six months she left, taking their young son with her.

After twelve years of flying solo, Glasheen placed an ad on an Internet dating site. "One of the last true adventurers!" Glasheen wrote on his profile, accompanied by a beaming photograph. "I need a woman with an adventurous spirit, a warm heart and an open mind. The type of woman I am seeking must be the kind who finds more joy in the beauty of nature, than in shopping malls or fashion. One who appreciates the serenity of living amidst nature, and who can put up with the peculiarities of life on a remote (yet accessible) island."

More than two hundred women responded. The *National Enquirer* did a feature on the "lovelorn Robinson Crusoe" and the story was picked up by newspapers around the world. The *New York Times* wrote about him for their Home & Garden section. He also appeared in a story in the Australian edition of *60 Minutes* about three guys who recreated Bligh's voyage. And last year Russell Crowe, who had learned about Restoration Island while researching a role as an eighteenth-century sea captain in the movie *Master and Commander*, stopped in for a pop.

Starry skies, fresh grilled fish, homemade brew, French chicks with lavender oil, and Russell Crowe pulling up with a vintage red—what could be better? Glasheen says he looks back at losing his fortune as a blessing. "I'm very attached to this land and I'm part of this land, I will die here," he said in an interview. But living in paradise comes at a price: Only a few of the women who answered his ad caught his fancy and, countless e-mails later, the search proved fruitless. "There is an inherent conflict between the peace of total solitude and the pleasures of companionship," he admitted in the *Times* story. "It's literally like living in heaven on Earth . . . but I guess I could say I'm desperately lonely sometimes."

Freya found him to be a bit of a sad sack. She had told me, several times, that although she didn't need friends and didn't feel comfortable around many people, she wanted and needed a life partner. Unlike Dave, however, she still fully expected to find one. While Freya kept proving that she could do anything she set her mind to, I admit I had my doubts about her strategy. She had chosen to spend a year on the move, far from home, in a country with more crocodiles than eligible bachelors.

CHAPTER SIX

Tropical Paradise

"The artist, like the idiot or clown, sits on the edge of the world, and a push may send him over it."

—SIR FRANCIS OSBERT SITWELL, *THE SCARLET TREE*

SEEN FROM ABOVE, CAPE YORK LOOKS LIKE A GIANT DORSAL FIN POINTING north from Australia across the island-studded Torres Strait to Papua New Guinea. Bordered on the east by the Coral Sea and the west by the Gulf of Carpentaria, this heavily eroded, sparsely populated tropical savannah is dominated by meandering rivers, vast floodplains, and the Great Dividing Range, which runs along the east coast.

Occupied for thousands of years by seafaring Aboriginals known today as "sand beach people," the Cape is a land not easily penetrated by outsiders. In 1848, Edmund Kennedy, a tough-as-biltong British surveyor, was sent to find a route overland from Sydney to the Gulf of Carpentaria. A party of thirteen sailed from Sydney to Rockingham Bay, south of present day Cairns, and subsequently headed into the bush with twenty-seven horses and a flock of sheep. Bogged down by mangroves and swamps, crocs and mountains, one man fell critically ill, another accidentally shot himself, and six more starved to death. Kennedy took a spear in the back by the inappropriately named Escape River and died in the arms of his young Aboriginal sidekick, Jackey Jackey.

A century and a half later, there are only a handful of remote towns and a few hardscrabble dirt roads through the interior. If you time your visit right and have a good four-wheel-drive vehicle, you can bash across rivers and stream beds to the top of the Cape, but forget about visiting between November and April when the monsoons drop up to 8 feet of rain on soil so old and depleted that folks who study dirt classify it as "skeletal." And do try to avoid the handful of cyclones that touch down there each year.

All things considered, it's easy to see why an area the size of Florida would be home to only fifteen thousand people, most of them Aboriginals and Torres Strait Islanders. But if you've got a reason to go there—if you're a fisherman, pearl farmer, miner, escaped convict, or a woman circumnavigating Australia in an 18-foot kayak—you can't do better than Cape York.

Thirty-six miles north of Restoration Island, as the sun was melting into the sea, Freya paddled past a big shark and landed on Saunders Island. She sloshed through tidal pools hauling two large gear bags to a flat sandy spot above the high-water mark. As she hustled back to her kayak, her flashlight caught a shiny object at the water's edge. She thought it might be a stick with a beer can stuck on the end, which in Australia is a fairly common way to mark a landing through the reef. But as she came closer, she realized the reflection was a gleaming eye at the end of a "longish shadow."

Bugger! she thought as she turned tail, leaving the creature to his prehistoric thoughts. She crossed two slide marks on her way back to camp, about 100 yards up from the water. Unlike Sandy Robson, whose jangled nerves nearly powered her satellite phone, Freya felt confident that the croc would not give chase. As she put it later on her blog, "I simply knew that guy didn't smell food in me and wouldn't move his butt towards my tent."

She took what she thought was a reasonable precaution, dragging her boat between her tent and the water and zipping herself inside. Out of sight, out of mind. She boiled a bag of noodles ("upgraded" with nuts), inserted her ear plugs and slept till first light. "No scary feelings," she wrote. "And at least now I knew how they looked at night."

In the morning she paddled off at pace. "In case he was still sunning, I didn't want to disturb him."

— ~ —

Two days and 80 miles later, she rode a ripping current through the turbulent passage past Albany Island and there it was: the northernmost tip of the Land Down Under. It had taken Freya ninety-three days and 2,758 miles to get here—the distance from New York City to Los Angeles—and although she paused to photograph the sign on a rocky ledge, she wasn't particularly moved. When Captain Cook stood here on August 22, 1770, he raised the Union Jack, fired off a few volleys, and named the tropical peninsula after a deceased duke. Freya wrote, "The Cape was like Capes mostly are, quite unspectacular. Only a plain metal sign on a pole in a drum filled with concrete."

To her the northernmost point of Australia was as special as the second northernmost point, or the third. Her attention was already fixated on the vast expanse of open water she intended to cross and the unseen point 350 miles west where she aimed to get out. Rock climbers talk about a challenge on a route as a "problem" to be solved; using that parlance, Freya was about to take on the biggest problem of her trip. In 1982 Paul Caffyn had reached the same spot 110 days into his trip and considered his options: Take the shortcut across the Gulf of Carpentaria or stick to the U-shaped coastline. If you look only at the numbers—350 versus 1,200 miles—the shortcut is a no-brainer. But when the sage geologist factored in the six to eight days alone on the open sea that the crossing would require, he opted for the coast, even if he might meet a croc or two along the way.

Freya had done her own calculations. She was seventeen days ahead of Caffyn—a decent cushion, but one that she knew could evaporate with an injury or spate of bad weather. At this point in his trip, Caffyn was averaging 35.4 miles a day, more than a mile per day faster than Freya. She was ahead of him only because he had taken more rest days for foul weather and an infected elbow. If she made it across the top of the Gulf, she would be at least five weeks ahead of him.

This seemed like a big *if* to those of us following along. Greg Barton, e-mailed her. "Are you still considering a crossing straight across the Gulf? While it will be a lot longer, I hope that you opt to take the safer route and paddle around."

"I never considered NOT crossing!" she replied. "I don't want to have croc encounters every night in the Gulf."

An engineer by trade, Barton is a measured man, professionally and personally. "Trying to make a 350-mile crossing without thoroughly testing your sleeping arrangements in extreme conditions could result in big problems. When you're 100 miles from shore problems could become life threatening very easily. We're all pushing for you and want to make sure you make it safely."

"Thanks for the concern," she fired back, "as long as your boat is not dissolving in 7 or 8 days afloat, it will be alright."

And that was the end of that conversation. A few days later, Jacqui King of Epic Oz sent the following e-mail to her colleagues:

The good news is that I have spoken to Cairns Water Police and they said they will contact her before she leaves Cooktown. They are going to discuss her itinerary, try and advise her and they will notify the Cape stations so they can keep tracking her. . . . He asked if Freya had personal insurance—and then said that a search and rescue operation would cost a phenomenal amount of money—the implication being that someone may have to foot the bill. The not-so-good news is he said they were not confident she would make it to the Cape. He said they've had 25 knot winds for two weeks and that it will blow nonstop until November. He also said that "we had a guy taken just recently" by a croc.

The officer had severe concerns about the amount of supplies she can carry on board. . . . They said her only chance of supplies are from passing commercial vessels and he doubted they would want to come to the party. I asked him about support vessels and he said that she would need a boat with sizeable fuel capacity because of the distance.

The person I spoke to at Marlin Marina said, "I cannot even think of one person who would entertain the idea." And . . . "if you did find *someone, it will cost gazillions of $'s because you would have to pay for the fuel there and back and it would have to be a very big boat." They offered to put a flyer up at the Marina if we sent one but added "we know every single boat owner in the area and if I asked them they would laugh and ask me if I was f**king mad."*

We have been released of legal liability and I can't see that we can do any more apart from sending someone to get the boat.

Cheers,
Jacqui

Named for a bigwig at the Dutch East India Company roughly thirty-nine thousand years after the first locals appeared in the area, the Gulf of Carpentaria is larger than all the Great Lakes combined with the state of Michigan thrown in. But its location is the reason the sea floor is littered with so many shipwrecks. Just above the north end of the Gulf, where Freya would be crossing, the Coral, Timor, and Arafura Seas funnel through the narrow straits between Papua New Guinea and Australia, creating constant turbulence. To complicate matters, the Gulf is shallow—it was part of a land bridge to Indonesia until the last Ice Age—which means even a relatively modest wind will kick up short, steep waves, and a shift in wind direction can change the direction of the swell, causing the water to erupt in confused, clashing waves. Oh yes, and it's a breeding ground for tropical cyclones.

It's worth noting that Caffyn wasn't averse to all open-water crossings. In 1979, the year before he and Nigel Dennis became the first paddlers to circumnavigate Great Britain, he and Max Reynolds crossed the Foveaux Strait—140 miles of open water between New Zealand's South and Stewart Islands, another first. He had also twice tried (and failed) to cross the Tasman Sea, roughly 1,000 miles of raucous water. And yet he chose not to attempt crossing the far shorter Gulf. For Freya, the distance across the Gulf was four times longer than her two previous open-water crossings combined.

So what. "I have a system," she told me in an e-mail from Cooktown. "I'm not scared. I will be fine."

It was a classic case of "*Vasdaproblum.*" She focused on the fact that three people had crossed the Gulf by kayak; therefore, it could be done. It didn't seem to matter that all three had suffered mightily. In 1993 Eric Stiller and his partner launched from Booby Island at the top of the Gulf in a two-man Klepper kayak with a sail. Stiller's worst fears were realized just hours after they hit open water and the chop grew like Jiffy Pop on a campfire. The conditions were unlike anything they had experienced in their previous 3,000 miles. In *Keep Australia on Your Left,* Stiller writes: "Waves came across *both sides* of the boat and *over the front*, with dump from the back . . . holding good lines on the waves and adjusting our bodies to every little nuance of the sea was torture."

Unable to sleep for the first fifty hours, he began hallucinating and struggled "to get some bearings in time and space, both of which had become vague, sometimes void." Though they had a sail up and were pushed by 15- to 20-knot westerly winds, paddling hardly a lick, by day three he was dehydrated and had no appetite. He shivered at night and struggled to take a shit during the day—although his bowels lurched each time he heard the kayak's frame creak in the rolling seas. His hands were swollen and covered in septic sores. The week was physical and psychological hell. When he took his first tentative steps after landing, his legs barely functioned. "I felt like an organism skipping links in the evolutionary chain to go from water to land. I got stuck on reptile. Higher thought processes would be a bigger jump still."

Freya had read Stiller's book. "I may simply pick a better weather window," she said.

More relevant to her effort was the solo, human-powered (no sail) crossing by Andrew McAuley. In the world of long-distance kayaking, McAuley, also an accomplished mountaineer and rock climber, was a big name—a meticulous planner who lived to pull off adventures that were, as he wrote on his blog, "unlikely and improbable." After warming up with three shorter crossings of the Bass Strait, the volatile stretch of water between southern Australia and Tasmania, he became the first person to do a direct, nonstop crossing of the Gulf of Carpentaria in 2004. He wrote, "It was the unknowns that made this trip attractive . . . No one knew how long this trip would take or even if it could be done."

Freya, of course, knew of McAuley; she had read about his Gulf crossing after he was named Adventurer of the Year by the Australian Geographic Society. When she was down around Melbourne she had met with two of his mates. One was Dave Winkworth, who probably paddled up north in croc country more than anyone alive. Winky had helped McAuley devise a sleeping system for the crossing. "Andrew found the trip very trying," he said.

McAuley was paddling along the coast the day before he was to start across when a shark struck so hard it lifted his kayak out of the water. The shark also sampled his rudder, bending it severely. McAuley mended the rudder on shore, a luxury he would not have once he was out to sea.

While his days were filled with the toil of paddling, the nights were the bigger challenge. He had removed the bulkheads from his boat so that he could lie down inside it—a setup Freya likened to sleeping in a coffin, and a wet and noisy one at that. Waves whacked the side of his boat and sloshed through the air vents: "It was like having someone throw a bucket of water on your face every ten seconds," he said afterwards in a radio interview. Halfway through his six-and-a-half day crossing, he wrote in his diary:

> *Last night was a rough night's sleep. Waves are constantly breaking over the top of my kayak and I had to get up and pump out the cockpit half a dozen times. After hours of this I resigned myself to sleeping in four or five inches of salt water and just decided to make the best of my miserable lot. . . . I have open sores and abscesses all over my body and every paddle stroke is incredibly painful. . . . So many people told me I was mad, and I'm now beginning to think that perhaps they were right. But I console myself with this thought: I've come this far, I'm still afloat, and it's a lot better than swimming.*

In February 2006, he and two mates did a 500-mile unsupported trip in Antarctica, going farther south than any sea kayak had ever been before. And then McAuley embarked on the trip that had intrigued him for years—a solo, unsupported crossing of the Tasman Sea from Australia to New Zealand in a conventional sea kayak, the trip Caffyn had not been able to complete. This 1,000-mile, rough-as-guts swath of the South Pacific known to locals as "The Ditch" had been crossed just once by a human-powered vessel; an English-born Kiwi transplant, Colin Quincy, took sixty-three days to row across in 1977. While this was a stunning achievement in its own right, a rowing dory is a virtual motor home compared to a conventional sea kayak.

McAuley shoved off in January 2007. After four harrowing weeks at sea, he was within 35 miles of his destination of Milford Sound in New Zealand, close enough to see the mountainous coastline, when he capsized, most likely from a rogue wave. His kayak was recovered but his body was never found.

It was both remarkable and maddening that Freya was able to take in what was useful to her from McAuley's experience and yet remain impervious to the fact that while he had survived his Gulf crossing, he had died on the next one. When McAuley was asked in an interview prior to his Tasman trip how, as a husband and the father of a young son, he could justify the kinds of risks he took, he said: "I try to cover all bases and be as prepared and skilled as possible, because when you do these things you are exposing yourself to criticism . . . I take risks, but they are calculated risks. I want to be beyond criticism."

Perhaps through preparation and skill, McAuley had reduced his risk from (pick a number) a one-in-five chance of dying to a one-in-ten chance. To him, that was a huge difference—to a normal person, that's still a one-in-ten chance of dying. I watched the National Geographic Channel documentary of his journey, *Solo: Lost at Sea*, which uses video footage recovered from the one surviving memory stick in his video camera and interviews with people on his support team.* The film begins with the garbled distress call he made on February 9. We see him weeping uncontrollably when he says good-bye to his wife and son and we get an inside-the-cockpit view of

---

* To see for yourself, go to: http://topdocumentaryfilms.com/solo-lost-at-sea.

the Tasman Sea being very big, cold, and scary and the exhausted and ashen thirty-nine-year-old being tiny, vulnerable, and brave; it seemed a minor miracle that he had survived as long as he did.

Before I watched the film, I envisioned McAuley handling the stress of the voyage with courage and calm. But seeing the fear and fatigue in his eyes, hearing his resolve give way to resignation, his bold mission seemed less of an exploration into the unknown and more like an addiction gone awry. It left a wife crippled by grief and a son who would never know his old man, and it was hard not to feel anger and think of McAuley as part clueless hammerhead, part narcissist.

Freya, of course, also had a son. While she seemed to care not at all about criticism, her fundamental approach to crossing the Gulf was the same as McAuley's: minimize risk to the extent you can and then just go. And be 100 percent confident you'll make it, all evidence to the contrary. I understood why Freya would not have wanted to watch the documentary before her own trip. What was harder to take was her telling me that, while she had no interest in doing a crossing as long as the Tasman herself ("I'm a Taurus, an Earth sign; I need to see land occasionally"), if she ever *did* tackle it, "I'd survive!"

⌐＊＾

As Freya's crossing drew near, the online buzz grew louder. Her regular blog readers, always enthusiastic, crossed over to worshipful, as if they were writing to Joan of Arc before her march on Orleans. This contrasted sharply with the e-mail and Skype chatter among those of us who viewed her preternatural confidence as willful ignorance rather than an inspiration. Early on I had seen her cockiness and nonchalance as potentially fatal flaws, but as she had moved seamlessly up the coast over the past one hundred days, meeting every challenge without a word of complaint, I found it increasingly difficult not to admire her tenacity and guts. So the Gulf crossing was a welcome excuse for my petty side to get back on its high horse. Who was she to ignore the advice of those who knew better, not to mention Paul Caffyn's example? And it irritated me that she kept referring to a 350-mile-wide inland sea as a "millpond."

Oscar, who had warned Freya repeatedly about the crossing, called with a renewed intensity. One day he predicted sleep deprivation would do her in; the next day, a storm; then, of course, there was the combination of the two. "She might survive three or four days," he opined, "but if a storm moves in and she's exhausted, she's fucked!"

Even accounting for the O Factor—as a rule of thumb, all his statements are 25 percent hyperbole—in this case he made perfect sense. How Freya expected to sleep in a boat 22 inches wide in a sea known for standing on its head was beyond me. Because her kayak was loaded for a much longer trip, she did not have the option, as McAuley did, of removing the bulkheads to sleep inside at night; she had fully packed compartments fore and aft of the cockpit. She planned to recline on the back deck, which would make the boat tippier and expose her to the elements—and to the tiger sharks that had dogged Paul Caffyn around the Gulf.

For a critic and a grudging fan, it was a most confusing time.

—◦—

Her first stop after rounding Cape York was the town of Seisia. A hulking supply ship was docked at a jetty that even at low tide stretched far into the bay. Seisia is one of five small indigenous communities (along with Injinoo, New Mapoon, Umagico, and Bamaga) in the Northern Peninsula. A family from an island south of New Guinea arrived on Red Island Point on a pearl lugger in 1947 and rechristened the spot Seisia, a word made from the first initials of the names of their six sons. (OK, if you must know: Saguakaz, Elu, Isua, Suni, Ibaui, and Aken.) Although there are just 184 residents, Seisia serves the commercial fishing industry and has a petrol station, taxi service, and a well-stocked supermarket—and, according to the caretaker at the camp where Freya pitched her tent, plenty of crocs. Standing in the midday sun, the clear blue water called her name but the sign on the beach was equally clear: CROCODILES ARE IN THE AREA, NO SWIMMING IN THE WATER.

After a "looong, lovely shower," Freya shaved her legs, painted her toenails red, slipped into her ten-ounce, silky black sleeping bag liner (which doubled as a sundress), and headed straight to the camp store for ice cream and potato chips—"essential" foods after weeks of dehydrated fare. The illusion of glamour was somewhat strained by the tan lines that made each bulging bicep look like a black and white cookie, but she headed down the wharf "feeling like a normal woman again."

She went to the post office to pick up the food parcel she had shipped from Cooktown. The clerk told her that if she was serious about paddling across the Gulf, she should talk to Greg Bethune, the captain of a sport fishing charter. "Greg knows the Gulf better than anyone," he said.

Why not? She found the fifty-one-year-old skipper down on the wharf loading provisions on to *Tropical Paradise*, a spiffy 62-foot cruiser that could sleep twelve. Six feet tall with brown eyes and straight brown hair, he wore a pair of reading glasses around his neck. He wasn't a washboard abs kind of guy, but he possessed the hardy good looks of a man who works outside because he wants to. Although he wasn't a big talker, somewhere between him showing her his tide charts and extending an invitation to dinner, the Woman in Black raised a plucked eyebrow and thought, "This could be interesting. . . ."

What a setup, eh? When Freya arrived for their date, the skipper had just stepped out of the shower. It seems inevitable that he would escort the sexiest woman in sea kayaking to the top deck, where they would sip champagne under the stars and, against the distant strains of a didgeridoo, ponder the vicissitudes of risk, loneliness, and love.

But it was not to be. Why not? "I hate men with wet hair," she told me, adding that he wore a tank top that revealed a tad too much paunch. So while Freya enjoyed Bethune's fresh fish and culinary skills, after dinner she headed back to her tent. They had made a tentative date to meet again down by the Jackson River, but only because he was taking his clients there to fish and she planned to pass by en route to Jantz Point, a bump in the coast that would trim 34 miles and about one day from the crossing. She thought that refilling her water bags on his boat would be "a convenient option."

Freya spent the next day in Seisia, organizing gear, napping, and cursing the shaky Internet connection. She left early the following morning and arrived at Vyrlia Point just before dusk, 20 miles shy of Jackson River. It was a 40-mile day made far tougher by the "bloody bitch of a wind." The following day, as she paddled south, she summoned Greg on the VHF radio. "I need to head out your way," he told her, "I'll buzz by to see you."

He arrived in a small motorboat, standing at the helm behind a stack of crab pots. This time he wore a baggy shirt and was as dry as the mackerel mounted on his office wall. As their boats drifted together, he extended his hand to her, smiling broadly. The moment she felt his powerful grip she knew she would spend the night on the *Tropical Paradise,* dine on fresh crab, and sleep between clean sheets. In the morning she would start the crossing. She abandoned her plan to leave from Jantz Point. The weather forecast was promising and she was ready now.

Energized by the decision, she repacked her boat on the beach at Jackson River in a cloud of angry red flies, making sure all the food and water she needed for the next ten days was either in the day hatch, behind her seat, or stowed on deck. "No need to open the front or back hatch," she said.

Sea kayaks, while enormously seaworthy, are by nature coastal vessels. They want to find a dock at night. They give the paddler no shelter from the elements and no place to sleep, and virtually all of the big human-powered open-water crossings have been done in vessels modified to correct these limitations. Venturing far out to sea in a traditional kayak is the paddling equivalent of . . . what? Hang-gliding across a desert for a week? Riding a bike on a plank across a very, very large snake pit? The day before he headed into the Gulf, Andrew McAuley said, "It's a very intimidating thing to stand on the beach and look out across the west and . . . there's just water everywhere. There's a bit of soul-searching involved."

Freya had no such concerns. Shortly before she launched, she wrote: "I'm heading out in good spirits, not scared at all about what would be ahead of me! Full of energy and motivation." She did acknowledge the risk—at least I think she did: "Shortcuts, though harder and more dangerous, are just my nature, punching through the wall, head first and eventually reaching the goal sooner than later!"

On the other hand, she seemed to have slept poorly the night before. Could it be she was human after all? "My rest on the boat could have been better as I was not used to the engine running all night. And maybe my mind was a bit busy with the crossing already to sleep deep and peacefully."

I felt genuinely worried for her. Three very strong paddlers had preceded Freya to the Gulf: a kayak instructor from New York who had been reduced to walking like a geriatric reptile; a professional adventurer who likened his Gulf crossing to "going 15 rounds with Mike Tyson"; and the living legend who became the first man to circumnavigate the continent. Call me a wimp, but considering their CVs—and the fact that Caffyn is still alive and McAuley is not—I would have followed the legend who took the long way around.

Forget the fact that I have a hard time sleeping if my cat decides to play with a pipe cleaner in the early hours of the morning. I felt Freya's greatest challenge on the crossing would be getting enough rest to function. And here she was, poor thing, wracked with anxiety, starting with a deficit.

But as it turned out, she hadn't told her fans the whole story of that last evening. At dinner Freya and Greg's eyes kept meeting across the crowded table of ravenous fishermen. When she excused herself on the grounds that she had to get up early for the big launch, the hospitable captain escorted her to her cabin, which coincidentally was adjacent to his. He stood in the narrow doorway and politely offered a goodnight kiss. She demurred. "My lips are too sunburned," she said, "but you could massage my neck."

It was the start of a long night of very little sleep.

The first rays of light streaming through the porthole found them still awake, lying in bed holding hands. Her neck felt much better and as for the rest of the massage, well, she thought, "I wouldn't mind seeing him again."

In other words, it wasn't nerves that had kept Freya Hoffmeister up the night before the crossing.

CHAPTER SEVEN

Maximum Wetness

"I am Sisyphus and the stone which I push up the mountain is my own psyche."
—REINHOLD MESSNER, THE FIRST MAN TO CLIMB MOUNT
EVEREST ALONE AND WITHOUT SUPPLEMENTAL OXYGEN

FEELING SURPRISINGLY REFRESHED AFTER JUST TWO HOURS OF SLEEP, Freya paddled down the Jackson River with Greg trolling alongside in his motorboat, talking about a possible business plan. "Would kayakers hire a charter to take them to exotic places to paddle around the Gulf?" he asked. She assured him they would. They reached the mouth of the river and the Gulf unfolded before them like a vast canyon. Freya gazed out at the water for a moment before turning back to Greg.

"To make it work," she said, "you will need a good guide."

He smiled. "That would be you."

She would have plenty of time during the next week to think about what that meant. But daylight hours were precious and with a quick kiss goodbye she was off to Nhulunbuy, 357.3 miles across the Gulf. It had been a productive stop. She had tanked up on water, enjoyed a sumptuous fish dinner and a thorough massage, and been offered a job on a fishing charter. You would never guess we were in the middle of a global recession.

Greg had spent enough time with Freya to see that she was well equipped; he trusted her competence and figured that if she got lucky with the weather she would be OK. But as he watched her recede in the distance like a vanishing dot on an old television, "I did think I might be the last person to see her," he said later.

— ◦ —

By 7:00 p.m., she had covered 43.5 miles. At this pace she figured she would reach Nhulunbuy in eight days.

It was time to set up her sleeping system, a paddle strapped across the boat behind the cockpit, with inflatable floats over each blade. This giant Q-tip would serve as an outrigger to stabilize the craft when she wasn't paddling. When she tested the system before arriving in Cairns she got seasick, but it still seemed the best of her very few options. She had thought about using two paddles—one fore and one aft of the cockpit—but after conducting a dry land test of this setup in Cairns she decided the boat would be sufficiently stable with just one. As the setting sun bathed the sedate Gulf in fiery shades of red, she passed a Thule strap under the boat with the paddle still in front of her, a tough task made easier by the balance and flexibility she had acquired as a gymnast and never lost. Looking on the bright side, it was a lot less trouble than setting up camp on land.

The chill grabbed her as soon as she stopped paddling. She slipped a long-sleeve fleece top and long neoprene pants over her wet paddling clothes, replaced her sandals with neoprene socks ("Do you go to bed with shoes?" she asked rhetorically on her blog), wrapped a scarf around her head, and covered the whole damp ensemble with a waterproof Gore-Tex "overcag"—a one-piece, thigh-length hooded jacket and spray skirt combo. She snapped a few pictures of her get-up for posterity, in which she looks like a hydrophobic monk. She slurped a package of pre-cooked Uncle Ben's rice with extra tuna and mayo, called Greg on the satellite phone ("just a quick hello to say I was OK") and by 8:00 p.m. she was ready for bed.

Using her life jacket and Thermarest as a mattress and pillow, she stretched her legs out into the cockpit, spread her arms along the paddle shaft, and drifted off to sleep. The secret to her success, she reported proudly, was the third, half-inflated float she put on the seat to lift her body. "This way I had padding for my sore bum and my back was not bent on the back deck. I could even turn my body a bit sideways on the float to change position sometimes. I was wet all over but still 90 percent warm, softly padded, stable, nice thoughts on my mind, so why not get some good sleep?" All she was missing was neoprene gloves, which she would have taken even over warm milk and chocolate chip cookies.

Early Saturday morning Australia time, Freya contacted Chris Cunningham on her satellite phone and gave him her GPS location. He posted a brief message on her blog:

> *The swell last night was bigger than she expected . . . Wind Beaufort 4 or 5 [14–24 mph]. She got some rest and drifted 10km [6.2 miles] overnight, fortunately in the right direction. Wind is easing this morning and she is underway. She is counting down kilometers and has 490 km [304.47 miles] to go.*

I found the report oddly unsatisfying. True, it was skimpy on details, but I had a sneaking suspicion that I was disappointed nothing more exciting had happened. Still, I had read enough to know that winds that strong—up to 24 mph—would typically rile up the Gulf like a stone thrown at a hornets' nest. So maybe "bigger than expected" was Freya-speak for pretty darn big. And it seemed likely that "some rest" would become "no rest" soon if the wind carried on.

The crossing had generated a sharp uptick in the daily number of hits on the site, as the more casual followers went into "holy-shit-she's-really-doing-this" mode. I never got around to watching *Survivor*, but I can't imagine that any reality TV show could be more gripping; after all, Freya had no producers or medical staff to step in should things go pear-shaped. The next day I checked her website compulsively until Cunningham's message finally appeared under a little Google Earth map with a yellow push pin showing her precise location on the big blue expanse that was the Gulf. He informed us that not only had she once again drifted in the right direction, but she had made her "comfy" bed softer still and, incredibly, had "slept like a baby" and awakened "full of energy." Similar messages followed after nights three and four.

How annoying! Here I had been fretting like my Grandma Hattie while this crazy German was snoozing in the middle of the Gulf of Carpentaria like a babe in her father's arms. Of course I didn't want her to die, but the spectator in me wanted a little more drama. And maybe the self-righteous dickhead in me didn't want the trip to be so easy, because that would make her right and all of us naysayers wrong.

Speaking of dickheads, by this time Oscar was calling twice a day on Skype. "She's flippin' lucky!" he shouted into my headset, "Wait till it blows 30 knots. She'll shit herself!"

This time I disagreed. "No, she won't—she's impervious to fear, Oscar. She's friggin' unbelievable."

As he ranted on, I flashed back to a calm, clear, moon-lit night on Lake Oahe, a 231-mile-long reservoir on the Missouri River that spans South and North Dakota. I was midway through a 2,700-mile trip from eastern Montana to Chicago and decided to take advantage of the perfect conditions and paddle through the night. When I ran out of steam around 1:00 a.m., I tied my boat to a downed tree far off shore and passed out, only to wake an hour later to crashing thunder and lightning.

Did I shit myself? Like an elephant on Raisin Bran. It took me two frantic hours to paddle into the wind and whitecaps to the safety of the leeward shore. But it was just one night—OK, half of one night—and I've been talking about it ever since. Freya had already been out for four days, alone, in the ocean, in big wind.

"Oscar, give her some credit," I said. "She's sleeping on the back of a kayak like an executive flying first class."

Of course, attitude is everything. One reason Freya was sleeping so well is because she chose to think of it as sleeping well. Another person faced with the same challenges to somnolence (me, for example) might have put a different spin on the experience. Here is a short list of what Freya's first four nights—the "easy" nights—involved:

The Drift Factor: Every two hours Freya opened one heavy eyelid to check her position on the GPS. She didn't drop a sea anchor because she was drifting west and cutting down miles even if she went slightly off-bearing. But that meant she had to monitor her position like a night watchman making rounds.

The Sea Snake Factor: Big, thick, long sea snakes, some swollen with fish in their bellies, slithered by with frightening regularity. One night she paddled an hour or two past sunset, but the snake sightings were so frequent she stopped. "I didn't want to flip a snake into my lap when I couldn't see."

The Fish Feeding Factor: Before "turning in" each evening Freya stopped to set up her paddle floats. The entire process took just three minutes but during the time she "was floating helplessly" she got seasick and puked. On the bright side, it only happened three times and only at dusk.

The Dangle Factor: Freya slept with her arms outstretched along the paddle shaft and her hands on the floats at each end to keep the paddle from rotating and increase the boat's stability. In some part of her sleeping brain she had to keep her hands from slipping off the paddle into the water "so as not to feed the big fish."

The Free Parking Factor: During the night birds landed on her with surprising regularity. "They probably thought I was a great log floating in the water!"

The Flying Fish Factor: Flashing inches above the water like slimy UFOs, flying fish smashed into her. When one hit her face "it left a stinky, fishy spot which kept me awake."

The Crick Factor: As she drifted without a sea anchor, her boat floated parallel to the waves. "To avoid taking waves in the face, I turned my head in one direction only."

The Oxygen Factor: To protect her face from rain and spray, she cinched the hood of her Gore-Tex jacket tight over her face. The trick was to leave enough room to breathe. "I pulled my neoprene visor over my eyes and only my nose stuck out." While a pert nose is an advantage in a beauty contest, it lacks the hood clearance of a real schnozzola.

The Oh Shit Factor: When the wind kicked up, big waves that she dubbed "lovely breakers" would crash over her head every ten minutes or so—just far enough apart so she could fall asleep in between. "If I could hear them coming I could turn my face away, but sometimes I was really fast asleep!"

On the plus side, there was a near-zero possibility of a boat running into her in the dark. There were no boats. And, consequently, no chance of rescue should she run into trouble.

On day five she passed the halfway mark—189.5 miles down; 167.7 to go.

After logging more than 3,000 miles over the last one hundred days, Freya had calluses in all the right places. Still, she knew that McAuley had suffered open sores and abscesses all over his body, and did what she could to avoid them, using pads and clothing to minimize rubbing. She developed pimples on her face from wearing sunscreen all day ("next time I'll have some scrubby stuff handy!") and red welts sprang up on her calves. But she suffered only "a slight bit of chafing in the butt fold where the permanently wet skin rubs against each other and this was not bothering me on sitting or paddling at all."

Here her focus, attention to detail, and ability to spend endless hours in the boat were essential. "Caring about your personal needs on such a crossing requires some good balance," she said. "You should be able to eat, drink, pee, put on shoes and change your shirt or pants without putting up the stabilization floats first." She had long ago abandoned her funnel for the simpler practice of peeing in the cockpit: "There is some water in the cockpit anyway all day from paddling. After a pee, you squeeze fresh water over your crotch and sponge or pump everything out of the cockpit. If it's too rough, the job simply has to wait."

New was dealing with "No. 2." But, as she proudly told me, "I was even able to do that without floats the first day! But it was calm. It's definitely more relaxing with stabilization floats." I would have thought the best approach would be simply to jump in the water when nature called. She found the idea of sharing the ocean with her own poop too icky, but there was also the possibility of sea creatures being attracted, food-wise, to one or the other of them (the lady or the poop). "No way," she said. "I simply got my legs out of the cockpit, lifted my butt off the seat, stripped my pants down, and took care I was aiming well on my removable seat pad. It was easy to empty it overboard and to wash it and me clean then."

To each his own, said the farmer as he kissed the cow. When people asked Ed Gillet how he dealt with this on his California to Hawaii crossing, he joked that he saved it all up in a BIG garbage bag.

To break up the monotony, she called Chris Cunningham in the morning and Greg Bethune at night. She chatted occasionally with her mother and son. She sang "silly folk songs." She talked to herself. ("Am I getting a slight bit odd?" she wrote in her blog afterwards.) She fantasized about "previous and upcoming" lovers. ("It was perfect, I can tell you. Very comfortable, and you can scream as loud as you like.")

While Freya was extremely open about her bodily functions, I was unable to get her to discuss the psychological impact of spending eight days alone in a place Eric Stiller dubbed "maximum wilderness." It was fine because she was fine. "If you are not happy with and by yourself," she said, "you better not go on such a trip. The remoteness of Australia may be the worst for the most social paddlers."

Of course, going solo distinguished her from the man whose record she was chasing. "Twenty-seven years ago," she said, "Paul Caffyn did well on having a support crew driving with him most of the time and he even had some different friends paddle some of the legs with him." But there was more to it than that. While for another paddler the solitude of the Gulf would be something to be, at best, endured, I suspected it actually appealed to her. The unrelenting severity of each day, and some days, each minute, continually confirmed what she had known all along—that she was mentally tougher than the rest. She gathered strength from this knowledge as the days passed.

During the fifth night the wind became a force, blowing out of the east at 20–30 knots. Sleep was all but impossible. The next day she napped intermittently, like a cat stuck in a tree, and covered just 34 miles, the fewest of the crossing so far. That night the heavens opened and she was enveloped in a torrential downpour. "Until you experience a tropical rain on the water," she said, "you can't imagine what it feels like." Unless you happen to have jumped out of an airplane during a rainstorm, something

Freya had done a few times in her skydiving days. "When you're free fall-ing faster than the drops, it seems as if the rain is coming from the earth instead of the sky. It actually hurts."

Bundled up in her tiny white boat, she rode the enormous swells roll-ing in slow motion toward the unseen shore as "heavy water drops poured down for hours out of a black sky." The long soak worsened the open sores on her knuckles, but she chose to accentuate the positive: "If you are in your kayak, wet anyway, what does it matter? The wind with the rain squall makes it just more of an experience!"

In other words, you don't paddle across the Gulf of Carpentaria expecting—or even hoping for—a smooth ride. Jonathan Borgais, the veteran sailor who provided McAuley with daily weather updates on his Tasman crossing, said, "I love the elements. When the weather gets harsh . . . it is like dancing with the sea. You merge with it. It is spiritual rather than physical."

Freya only became concerned when the prevailing easterly wind turned to a westerly, increased to 30–40 knots, and—as she lay in the rain trying to sleep—began to shove her backwards. For the first time in six days she deployed her improvised sea anchor—an open gear bag at the end of a rope attached to the toggle on the kayak's bow handle with a carabiner. The bag would act like a water parachute, slowing the boat to a near stop. "It worked well," she said. In fact, it worked so well that she feared it would exert so much force on the toggle that it would snap. She decided to tie the rope directly to the bow handle, but she needed to pull up the anchor to create enough slack so she could work with the rope. The problem was getting there—her regular paddle was strapped to the back deck and her spare stowed in a bag behind. So she hand-paddled. "It was tough to move forward with my whole paddle float sleeping setup," she said, but she finally reached the float on the rope, hauled up the bloated bag (checking carefully for snakes), crawled up front to the bow of the kayak, and re-tied the anchor directly to the handle. Then she lay back down and waited for the next wave to drop on her head.

Although she had solved one problem, she now started thinking about another. Her boat was lightweight carbon fiber, designed for speed and distance—what if the handle didn't hold? If it snapped there would be a "gaping, ugly" hole on the deck, at night, in rolling seas. The sea anchor slowed her backward progress, but it also pointed her directly into the wind. An assembly line of "big, fat breakers," some two stories high, rumbled her way. Without the sea anchor the boat had been side-on to the swell, so she could turn away when a hissing wave neared, but facing forward "I was getting the fat splash directly on my nose!!!"

With her hands spread on the floats all night, she could feel the force of the waves bending and flexing the paddle shaft, "like the waves were inside the paddle." At some point she pulled the spare paddle out of its bag on the back deck to have it handy in case the other one snapped. When she called Greg that night the connection was so bad it was impossible to talk. He posted a brief note on her website: "I did get that last night was very rough; the worst yet. She said she was OK, but I think she is incapable of complaint."

Finally, around 4:00 a.m., Mother Nature called off the dogs. The wind eased and the sea subsided. Better yet, Freya noticed a change of the drift direction toward the west. For the second time that night, she hauled in the anchor. Exhausted by her vigil, she lay back for two hours of blissful sleep.

On Thursday evening—the end of day seven—she sent Cunningham a text via satellite phone: "7th night out. 90km left. Will arrive Saturday."

But that morning she called Cunningham again, who reported: "I just got a satellite phone call from Freya. She got some sleep last night and . . . picked up 10 km of good drift overnight and added another 10 km paddling at night. She will be landing at Nhulunbuy tonight (Friday) somewhere around 6 pm to 9 pm. The Gove Surf Club and the town of Nhulunbuy is awaiting her arrival. Charles Rue [the head of the club] has alerted local air and sea traffic of Freya's progress so there are a lot of people keeping an eye out for her. She has a warm welcome awaiting her."

At midnight when she noticed she had drifted 3 miles in the right direction, she removed her sleeping system and resumed paddling. An hour later fatigue struck hard and she set up her floating camp again, snoozing until 5:00 a.m., an hour before first light. Once again, she had drifted another 3 miles closer to terra firma. Though the wind and rain returned, just 46 miles separated her and Nhulunbuy and she pushed on with renewed vigor, watching the kilometers fall away on her GPS and singing like a stupefied kid in the backseat of a car, approaching the end of an interminably long road trip.

With the cloud cover and rain, she was only 12 miles from shore when the twinkling lights of the surf club appeared in the grainy mist. Soon after, she saw the splash of paddle blades approaching. "I was happy and surprised, thinking that someone must have spotted me. Actually, Charles Rue went out on his surf ski, as he did most nights, hoping to find me somewhere in last light—a good omen, as I could have been much later arriving!"

It wasn't quite as momentous a meeting as Stanley and Livingstone, but it was thoroughly satisfying for both parties nonetheless. Rue showed Freya the way through the surf, riding the back of a wave along the concrete break wall to the surf club. A dozen arms reached out to help her from her boat but she waved them off and climbed out herself. She had not been on her feet once in the past eight days and she struggled a bit with her balance. But the inventory of her physical ailments was excessively short: "I developed ugly sore spots on my little toes on the last day . . . I noticed they were simply numb and very painful after stripping off my sandals."

The welcome at the club was fifty paddlers strong, "but the party was not really set up for me . . . it was simply Friday night's BBQ, and quite overwhelming after so many days out there by yourself! I must admit I'd rather have landed on a more quiet spot." Perhaps only Andrew McAuley could fully appreciate the physical and mental challenges Freya had endured. Of course I couldn't ask him what he thought about Freya choosing this high-risk shortcut across the Gulf, but I did read some of the articles written after his death. Dick Smith of the Australian Geographic Society offered a glimpse into the mind of a rapacious risk-taker like McAuley: "It's a selfish thing in many ways. Even though adventurers will tell you that it does have advantages of motivating other people . . . it is really something inside. An adrenaline-driving force that says: 'I can get away with it.' It's part of our psyche, part of evolution."

Patrick Spiers, a McAuley friend and mountain climber, said that when he leaves on a climbing trip, he's conscious "of the fear in the hearts of my family. I reassure them that if I am ever missing . . . I was out there in an environment I was seeking."

I also wrote to Lawrence Geoghegan, McAuley's paddling partner on his Antarctica trip. A wild-looking man with dreadlocks and the bushy red beard of a Viking, Geoghegan lives in a mud home he built in the town of Brogo off the Tasman Sea, where he manufactures sea kayaks using solar power. Dave Winkworth had suggested that Freya look him up when she passed through Brogo two weeks into her trip. He wrote: "A first attempt is always harder than second or third. Every other attempt has prior knowledge of the possibilities. If she found it easy and wasn't scared, good on her for saying that. But I don't believe a word of it."

I could imagine him thinking of his friend when I read his last line: "It might help sell her book, though."

CHAPTER EIGHT

Do Crocs Bark?

While you're certainly getting noticed in May, dear Taurus, there is a lot going on behind the scenes. A deliciously private love affair might figure this month, or you could be working on a creative project in solitude. Watch that you mean what you say, and say what you mean, because the likelihood of misunderstandings runs high. . . . Try to avoid situations that could lead to gossip.
—CafeAstrology.com, May 2009

A DIDGERIDOO CAN SOUND LIKE CROCS GROWLING IN AN ECHO CHAMBER, surf crashing on soft sand, or frogs croaking in a phone booth. It also evokes snakes slithering through tall grass, agitated parrots, water buffalos rutting, and Ike Turner's background vocals on *Proud Mary*. It's the outback during the day and, in the next circular breath, the cacophonous chatter of mangroves, tidal rivers, and a tropical forest at night—punctuated by an ocean liner's foghorn as it comes to port. Incredibly, you hear each element individually and all at once. If you don't believe me, paddle to the Top End of Australia, where, back when Christ was in nappies, the Yolngu People turned a eucalyptus branch hollowed out by termites into the world's first wind instrument. And where they continue to play it, with incredible virtuosity, today.

When Freya stepped out of her boat on the far side of the Gulf, she was in Arnhem Land, a vast, sparsely populated region in the Northern Territory that is one of the largest Aboriginal reserves in Australia. It may have been where Australia's indigenous people first arrived fifty thousand years ago, somehow managing to sail from Indonesia across 60-plus miles of open ocean tens of thousands of years before anthropologists have any reason to believe that humans knew enough about sailing, navigation, or even the Earth to make such a journey possible. Given this, it's natural to assume "Arnhem" is an Aboriginal word meaning *wrong again, white man.* But in fact it was the name of the Dutch ship that explored the jagged coast in 1623, affixed to the early map of Australia by none other than Matthew Flinders.

Freya took four days to recover from her arduous crossing, resting hard in Nhulumbuy in the William Gove House—free digs courtesy of the mining company that put the town on the map in the 1970s. Her swollen hands and feet returned to their normal size and the open sores on her calves and toes scabbed over. Once she had updated her blog, had her hair cut and restored to its former black luster, and painted her toenails shiny red, she was good to go. Early in the morning on May 6, she paddled through low muddy surf toward the most desolate stretch of her trip so far. Darwin, her next big stopover, was 500 miles west—fifteen paddling days away by her estimation.

It was slow going. Freya spent hours each day beating against a powerful tide pushing out of Brown Strait. Two days out of Nhulumbuy she landed on the northeast side of Elcho Island as the sun was setting. Before the light died she had to make a quick decision about where to camp: on high ground, on a path covered with water buffalo tracks and fresh dung, or down on the beach, closer to the crocs. Freya had yet to see a water buffalo, but she had been warned that they were dangerous and unpredictable. Introduced into the country from Timor in the 1800s to provide food and labor for white settlers, these former beasts of burden had long since gone feral.

They also weigh up to fifteen hundred pounds and have horns 5 feet across. With no fresh croc tracks visible on the beach, Freya opted for the low ground and the soft sand. After all, if a croc should make its way toward her camp, there was always the chance that it would encounter a wandering water buffalo. If it was a large male croc, it surely would choose a ton of beef over 160 pounds of human. Problem solved.

Freya's strategy to minimize croc contact on the east coast had been to stay far off shore, camping on remote islands in the Great Barrier Reef. But in Arnhem the coastline didn't lend itself to that approach, and she was far closer to river mouths, estuaries, and the narrow channels favored by these ancient predators than she had been so far. Although she had planned to paddle around to the offshore (presumably less croc-y) side of Elcho Island to camp, she had run out of light before she got there. One of Freya's great strengths as an expedition paddler is her ability to not waste energy worrying about something that might not happen. She didn't even use her boat as a barricade as she had in the past; because she was so close to the water she chose to tie it to a tree up on the beach to keep it safe. She slept well and paddled off early the following morning without incident.

I had to wonder—were I in her shoes, which risk would I choose? Given the number of horrifying croc stories I had heard since Freya announced her trip in Hawaii, I doubted I would choose the beach. I decided to check with my best crocodile source, Dave Winkworth. By way of reply, he told me a story. He and a mate were paddling through these same Arnhem waters when Winky spotted a croc's snout 40 yards to his right. In the next breath the arched armor-plated back appeared on the surface, a sure sign of aggression. The men took off like sprinters at the starting gun. When Dave finally dared to look back, he saw they had opened a decent gap—crocs don't like to go very fast for very long. Completely drained, they landed on Elcho Island's mangrove-fringed beach for a "cuppa" to soothe their shaken nerves, only to find a telltale slide on the bank that shouted monster-large croc.

And that's where Freya had slept. I concluded that Winky would have been right up there on the high ground with me, fending off water buffalo. He told me that while he thought Freya had read his account of that trip before she came to Australia, when they met she wanted to focus on crocodile avoidance rather than cautionary tales. "I told her my main measure which is: Never ever put your paddle down if you see a croc while on the water. A paddle in your hands is speed, stability and a quick roll. And—though God help you if you ever get this close—a defense implement."

The following evening Freya landed on the southern end of Elcho near an Aboriginal settlement called Galiwinku. It was a moonless night, and as she lay back in her tent she felt uneasy. "I was quite a bit scared about crocs coming up," she wrote in her blog. "I actually heard a strange grumbly barking noise at night. Do crocs bark?"

In fact they do. Croc experts believe their bark is a form of communication with four distinct riffs: distress, threat, hatching (made by the newborns), and courtship. In other words, unless the bark is Junior calling for Mom or Stanley calling for Stella, there's a good chance it's bad news.

But Freya's luck held that night, and continued to hold as she proceeded through the—*hint, hint*—Crocodile Islands. Each night she scanned the beach with her flashlight for "glooming eyes in the water," set up her tent, positioned her boat according to the perceived threat and, lulled by the sound of the waves lapping on the beach, slept soundly.

When she woke on the morning of May 10, she was forty-five years old. Freya was delighted to find a patchy wireless signal courtesy of the Aboriginal community on nearby Milingimbi Island. She had expected that family members and friends would write to say *Alles Gute zum Geburtstag*. But there were literally hundreds of birthday greetings from people following her trip from around the world.

In a land where the locals drink kava and speak the related clan languages *Gupapuyngu* and *Djambarrpuyngu*, where the only effective modes of travel are boat, sea plane, or bone-jarring four-wheel drive, Freya sat under a swaying palm reading her mail on her Toshiba laptop, a grin stretched across her sunburned face. Finally, at 11:00 a.m., five hours after her normal departure, she headed off across the Arafura Sea to False Point, buoyed by the chorus of birthday well wishes resounding in her head.

❦

Freya Gerlinde Hoffmeister was born on May 10, 1964, in Heikendorf, a small town on the Baltic Sea in northern Germany. Her parents' marriage, she said, was "traditional" and her childhood "very protected, very pleasant. I can't remember anything bad." She shared a bedroom with her older sister Edda, but being bigger and stronger she dictated who put what

After competing as a gymnast and then in beauty pageants, by age 20 Freya had turned to body building. She says her secret to success was that while the other women just stood there and posed, she danced to the music like a gymnast doing floor exercises. © FREYA HOFFMEISTER

Freya with her son Helge, age eight, at home in Husum, Germany. He was twelve when she began her Australia trip. © FREYA HOFFMEISTER

A packing genuis, Freya carried 83 pounds of gear in her 55-pound kayak, not counting food or water. Fully loaded with Freya aboard, her boat generally weighed more than 380 pounds. © GREG BETHUNE

Warned repeatedly not to cross the 355-mile-wide Gulf of Carpentaria, Freya took the shortcut to all but guarantee she would eclipse Paul Caffyn's record. © FREYA HOFFMEISTER

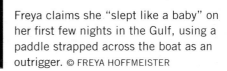

Freya claims she "slept like a baby" on her first few nights in the Gulf, using a paddle strapped across the boat as an outrigger. © FREYA HOFFMEISTER

Mid-trip break with Greg Bethune aboard the *Tropical Paradise*. She met the charter boat captain in April just before embarking across the Gulf and called him every day until they were reunited a month later for a week-long holiday.
© FREYA HOFFMEISTER

Though she was bumped by sharks many times, Freya was far more concerned about avoiding the saltwater crocs—until she was nearly knocked out of her boat by a shark on Day 175. Given the breadth of the bite marks on her stern, it was most likely a Great White.
© FREYA HOFFMEISTER

In parts of Western Australia, the tidal variation is as much as 28 feet—second only to the Bay of Fundy. When the tide went out, the ocean vanished, and Freya pulled her boat for miles along the coast. © FREYA HOFFMEISTER

When the tide returns, it comes back fast. Here Freya looks out over the mud flats of 80-Mile Beach, waiting. © FREYA HOFFMEISTER

Just minutes after Freya saw the water appear far off on the horizon, the boat was floating in milky white foam. © FREYA HOFFMEISTER

Freya's third goal for the trip—after completing it and setting a speed record—was to be known as the sexiest woman in sea kayaking. To that end, she posted photos on her blog displaying her feminine charms—such as this one of skinny-dipping in Mackay. FROM FREYA HOFFMEISTER'S COLLECTION

Freya sought to avoid the boat-crunching surf that defines much of the Australian coast by launching and landing behind headlands and through river mouths whenever possible. Still, she often had to bust out through multiple sets of big surf, a task made more difficult with a fully-loaded boat. Here she clears the shore break near Meerup in Western Australia. © TERRY BOLLAND

Timing is everything.
© TERRY BOLLAND

Made it, but just barely. © TERRY BOLLAND

Freya had to negotiate three sections of 100-plus miles of unbroken cliff faces. The toughest was the Zuytdorp Cliffs, which pushed her into "survival mode." Despite her exhaustion, she rolled her boat for the crowd as she finished.
© TERRY BOLLAND

Freya saw many whales during her trip, with one uncomfortably close encounter along the Zuytdorp Cliffs. This humpback, sadly, was stranded on a reef in southwestern Australia and not likely to survive. © FREYA HOFFMEISTER

Freya reached the Baxter Cliffs on Day 279 of her trip. Dangerously high winds forced her to wait for six days in the scorching heat. Seasickness and headwinds turned this second stretch of unbroken cliffs into another trying ordeal.
© GREG BETHUNE

The Bunda Cliffs, the third and final set. Note Freya's tiny kayak in the middle of the photo. © GREG BETHUNE

Three hundred thirty-two days and 8,565 miles after setting out from Caffyn Cove outside of Melbourne, Freya completes the circle. Her response after crossing the line was so nonchalant, a photographer asked her to back up and finish again. © GREG BETHUNE

Channeling her inner gymnast, Freya shows off for the crowd in Queenscliff. © GREG BETHUNE

where. Her mother was a primary school teacher who "always acted like a teacher." Her father, Dr. Heinrich Hoffmeister VII, a marine biologist, was the author of three books, the first a dry tome on fishing legislation, the second best described as the musings of a "forest man." He was a big man with a big personality. Freya adored him.

Anne-Marie Hoffmeister was a skilled seamstress and insisted on making most of the girls' clothes—jeans were verboten—which made them stand out in an un-cool, odd-duck sort of way. But she also led a popular tumbling class for tots and Freya was her ace student and model. "The kids loved it and I liked the attention," Freya said.

When she moved on to gymnastics school, she was bigger, broader, and more supple than the other girls her age. According to her sister Edda, now living in England with her husband and two children, "She was quiet and determined, and fearless." Before long Freya was one of the best gymnasts in her state, especially strong on the balance beam.

Pleasant indeed. But the longer we spoke about her childhood, the more apparent it became that there were a few cracks in her protected home. Her mother, Freya said, "was always the teaching type, instead of the loving type." A teacher with a temper. Squabbles between her girls were often settled with a large wooden cooking spoon or coat hanger.

Freya chalks it up to "small person syndrome"—her mother stood just 5'1". These beatings were about the extent of her physical contact with her mother. "I was never, ever physically close to my mother," she said. "She may have loved me but she wasn't able to show it. There's a picture of her hugging me as a kid but I can't remember any of that. When she watches me cuddle my son, she says, 'That's too much!'"

It was different with her father. They would often snuggle on the couch, and he liked to smell her hair. "He wasn't as affectionate as I was with my boy," she said, "but it was good enough to have good memories."

Dr. Hoffmeister was more relaxed and affable than Mrs. H. "He was secure within himself," Edda said. "He was successful. He had a good time at work and a good time outside of work. He was a much more rounded and balanced person." A sought-after speaker, he was often away from home.

Edda was by far the more outgoing and socially adept of the two girls; Freya had no close friends. "I'd rather be alone, even as a kid," she says. She had skipped first grade, and always being the youngest in her class made it even harder to fit in—had she wanted to fit in. She jumped headlong into sports. Her father, himself raised by a disciplined man who had been a lieutenant in the mounted cavalry during World War I, passed along to Freya the belief that she could—and should—excel in all arenas. She acquired so many trophies, medals, and certificates in so many physical pursuits that she could have been a Girl Scout on speed. "I always tried to be branded as outstanding," said Freya. "Every weekend I was bringing home a different certification. I never told my parents when I was reaching a new goal, but when I showed them the award they were always very proud."

At the age of sixteen, now too large to excel in gymnastics, she began practicing for her hunting license. In many states in America, all it takes to get a license to bag a buck is a nominal fee and proof that you've taken an online "hunter education program." But in Germany it requires a comprehensive six-month course, with a high failure rate. You take classes on the local wildlife and habitat and must demonstrate proficiency with a shotgun, rifle, and handgun. Freya remembers the shotgun test as particularly tense. To pass she had to nail three clay pigeons out of ten. She whiffed on her first seven shots; with each misfire she could feel her father's frustration mounting. "He urgently wanted me to pass," she said. Standing by was a high-ranking government official, a rival of her father's. "He urgently wanted me to fail," she said. But she blew away the last three targets and never looked back. She became a dead-eye with a .38 Smith & Wesson and her father, the president of the shooting club, beamed when she defeated men who smirked when they saw a girl lining up to compete.

Says Edda: "Being a strong, good German was important to my father and in this sense his expectations of his daughters were shaped by his political views . . . Freya's happiness came from triumph, winning, being the best. Because she knew it would win her approval from our parents."

While competition was the motivating force in Freya's life, it was also a wedge that divided the Hoffmeister girls. "My mother was always comparing Freya and me," Edda said. "She'd ask why I wasn't as neat as her. Or how come Freya wasn't as amiable as me. It became the constant refrain we lived with. Instead of teaching us to work together with tolerance she pitted us against each other, with predictable results."

Edda's view is that while she tried to ignore the competition, Freya embraced it. "We were constantly reminded that someone had to be better, and Freya had to be the one. Being constantly compared meant we were always fighting and my mother lost her temper very often and smashed the daylights out of us."

Edda frequently posted on Freya's blog; her notes were encouraging, supportive, sometimes concerned, and I just assumed the two sisters were close. But although Freya had started the blog for her Iceland trip, Edda says: "Until Australia, she never told us she had a blog." Edda had left home at seventeen; at eighteen she left Germany to travel abroad and communication between the two girls became perfunctory at best. They saw each other at infrequent family get-togethers, and even after Freya started traveling to the Anglesey Sea Kayaking Symposium in Wales she did not stop off to visit Edda and her family in England. Edda's blog posts constituted the most regular communication they'd had (one-sided though it might be) since they were girls.

After Edda moved out, the dynamic between Freya and her mother shifted. They were home alone one day and got into a spat about something. Freya spoke sharply to her mother and glanced up in time to see her poised to strike with the dreaded wooden spoon. This time Freya snatched the spoon and slammed it down. "That's the last time you'll ever hit me!" she shouted. And it was. "I wish she'd done that long before," Edda says.

Freya got her first pair of blue jeans when she was fifteen and her first boyfriend soon after that. He had a motorcycle and Freya bought a "sexy" red leather suit (to match her sexy red bike) so she would stand out among the black-leather crowd. "I liked to be outstanding in this way," she said. Her motorcycle mob toured around Germany and across Europe, riding during the day and partying around a bonfire at night. Freya drank hardly at all and "hated" smokers, but she loved going fast and found the sensation of speed so relaxing she would often fall asleep on the back of the bike with her cheek pressed up against her boyfriend's broad back.

Soon after she stopped competing as a gymnast, Freya accompanied her parents to a formal ball sponsored by the Department of Oceanography, where her father was a VIP. Despite the "horrible" brown leather skirt she was wearing, the statuesque sixteen-year-old was crowned the evening's "Prawn Queen." That's all it took. Freya went on the beauty pageant tour and took top honors at the city and state level. Heading into the Miss Germany contest she felt like a streaky hitter on a roll. A decade of gymnastics had taught her how to show off her body. "I have a strong physical presence when I walk into a room," she said, "an aura."

But presence and aura only get you so far. She finished sixth, which wasn't bad considering she hadn't invested in a talent coach or custom-made gowns—or slept with any of the judges, as she suspected a few of the girls who finished ahead of her had. She didn't care much. She was already on to her next big thing—bodybuilding.

Shortly after she had been named Miss Kiel, her boyfriend had dragged her to the gym. "I instantly loved it," she said. Gymnastics had sculpted her physique, and when she added iron to the mix her muscles responded like leavening bread. Bodybuilding combined discipline, strength, and sensuality and fit her like Cinderella's slipper. She enjoyed flexing in the mirror. She liked the feeling of pain in her muscles that meant she was making progress.

And she liked to be watched. Posing on stage next to a line-up of oily women smiling through gritted teeth, she found she could draw the crowd her way. While the other women "just stood there and posed" like pliable statues, Freya drew on her experience as a gymnast doing floor exercises. She danced to the music, seducing the judges like a buff belly dancer. "I got the biggest applause," she said, "people went crazy!"

She described this scene to me on a hot summer's day in New York City. Clad in a tight tank top, she twitched her pectorals like a horse shaking off flies. Chuckling, she said: "It's nice to get your titties jumping. Not many women can do that."

But, like beauty pageants, there was a seedy side to bodybuilding. Steroid use was rampant and she wasn't prepared to take drugs to move up to higher levels of competition. She quit the sport at twenty-one and has hardly touched a weight since.

Skydiving, her next passion, was less obviously about competition. But nor was it only about the thrill of falling through space. There were certifications to be earned, esoteric "firsts" to be claimed, like her tandem jump over the North Pole, and milestones to hit before she could quit (fifteen hundred jumps). It was the same with kayaking, the "tame" sport she turned to as a new mother. After establishing herself as the Greenland rolling champion, she set out to make a name for herself in expedition kayaking.

And to judge by the number of e-mails she received on her forty-fifth birthday, she had succeeded at that as well. After paddling 113 days and 3,335 miles along the coast of Australia, averaging 37 miles per day, Freya Gerlinde Hoffmeister had our complete attention.

After the excitement of the Gulf crossing, Freya's blog postings seemed a little pedestrian until the day she spotted a lone rock on the beach in the distance as she approached DeCourcy Head. It was a reddish, salt-encrusted pillar of stone—a good 10 feet tall—standing alone in the shore break on a deserted beach. A couple of boulders alongside and foamy white waves curling up the base completed the phallic portrait.

It was clear she found this surprise encounter with a petrologic hard-on a welcome distraction, at the very least. She posted two pictures of the "outstanding specimen" on her blog. Beneath one, she commented that it was "a bit over-sized, even for me being so lonely." Beneath the other, "Don't tell me I'm just needy and am having hallucinations . . ."

And then the wrap-up: "I surely had nice dreams last night with that mega-sized petrified penis beside me."

You could almost hear her most ardent male fans adjusting their spray skirts. Warren, a highly smitten devotee from the States, wrote: "No, Freya that's just me. I was working on my tan in the nude."

On Day 120, Freya left a "cute little island" off Ardigbiyi Point at 3:30 a.m., hoping to take advantage of the tide flooding through Dundas Strait. She stopped once to answer nature's more arduous call—"easily balancing while straddling the cockpit"—and once again "a fat shark" smashed into her stern with a startling jolt. "Good I had the paddle in my hands," she wrote, "as I had to brace."

Ten hours later, she landed on a spit of soft sand at Camp Point on the northeast side of Melville Island, Australia's second largest after Tasmania. There was a tranquil lagoon next to the river mouth surrounded by mangroves and casuarinas. It was so perfect that she couldn't bear to leave, even though she knew it was just the kind of place a crocodile would appreciate. She pulled her boat safely up the beach, stripped off her wet clothes, and walked out onto the spit to stretch her legs. When she saw no croc slides on the sand, she decided to take a quick dip in the freshwater lagoon. As she approached the water's edge, a dark log at the bottom floated to the surface, flashing a "friendly grin."

"It left me with goose bubbles on my skin for a while," she wrote. But having set her heart on a swim—something she had been avoiding since entering croc country—she walked to the ocean, jumped in, and quickly rinsed off. And there on the beach she saw evidence of another danger in paradise: water buffalo tracks—large and disturbingly deep. She took what precautions she could. She set up her tent behind a few downed trees and blocked the back side with her kayak. She left the tent windows open so she could check out any intruders. She had her camp stove and lighter nearby in case she needed to use it as a makeshift torch, and lay down with her paddle on one side and a sturdy branch on the other. By 6:00 p.m. she was snoozing hard.

Early the next morning, she worked on her blog for a few hours while waiting for the tide to turn and shoved off before 7:00. As she traveled along the glassy southeast shore of Melville Island, she passed Ant Cliffs, named by the British explorer John Lort Stokes, who came ashore in 1839 from the HMS *Beagle* (the very ship on which a young botanist named Charles Darwin had served from 1831 to 1836). Lort and his lads were standing under a tree when large green ants launched an "exceedingly painful" assault, forcing the men to tear off their clothes to "rid ourselves of these unwelcome visitors."

Freya's policy of never landing except to make camp at night kept her out of the way of the ants, but she was paddling in the muddy waters just off the cliffs when something smashed into the left side of her face—a big fish or a small croc?—with enough force to knock her over (and leave a bruise on her jaw for a week). She reached her destination for the day, Bonkalji Beach on the southern tip of Melville Island, shortly before sunset, only to find that the beach was littered with water buffalo prints. She had already paddled 31 miles, but, as she put it, "I simply didn't need my tent sliced by a curious bull's horn or some fat hoofs trampling over me and my gear." The forecast called for calm conditions. Even if Darwin was another 37 miles south, paddling all night across the Clarence Strait suddenly seemed like a great idea.

She set up her stove in the kayak's cockpit and fired up a pot of noodles. Between slurps, she organized her maps, programmed her GPS, called her contact in Darwin to say that she was ahead of schedule, and headed south. When darkness fell, she tracked the beams from the lighthouse on North Vernon Island 12 miles south until the hazy glow of Darwin appeared. A prawn trawler hauling its nets passed perilously near, jolting her out of a near doze. Paddling in Arnhem Land, it was easy to forget that such things existed. Around midnight a nasty headwind slowed her to a crawl. When it backed off she lay her head on the front deck for a cat nap. She sang to stay awake until she got close enough to Darwin to get cell phone reception. It was too late to call Greg, so she called her mother in Germany, many time zones away. Then she just counted down the miles on her GPS, drawn to the distant lights of civilization like a moth to a flame.

It was almost 4:00 a.m.—twenty-one hours and 68 miles after leaving Camp Point—when Freya pulled up on the flat sandy beach in front of the Darwin Surf Lifesaving Club. Almost on cue, the automated sprinkler system clicked on and she stripped off for an impromptu shower.

She set up her tent near the clubhouse, inserted earplugs, wrapped a scarf around her eyes, and fell fast asleep, supremely satisfied that Stage 7 was in the books. And although she was awakened two hours later by some misguided paddlers singing "Happy Birthday" outside her tent, she wasn't annoyed. She knew something they—and we—didn't know. She was taking a "halfway holiday"—ten days off—and it was starting now.

That afternoon she went shopping in Darwin, a city of 125,000 people, named after the botanist who introduced the world to the theory of evolution. She bought an airy red dress "to feel feminine again." Later that evening, she visited the Mindil Beach Sunset Market, a huge open-air market with food, crafts, and music that is a must-see for any traveler to Darwin. She took a picture of the Roadkill Cafe ("You Kill It, We Grill It") but passed on the kangaroo, buffalo, wallaby, camel, possum, emu, and crocodile that were on the day's menu.

And it was here, at the western edge of Arnhem Land, that she first heard a didgeridoo. The player was expert, but hardly Aboriginal. In fact, although he spoke English with a strong Aussie accent, his native language was German. His name was Mark Hoffman. Barefoot, dressed in baggy board shorts and sporting dreadlocks in a Mohawk, he and his drummer captivated the crowd. The party atmosphere was right in tune with both her sense of accomplishment and her anticipation of the week ahead. After the set she went up to Mark to buy a CD. When she told him her name, he laughed. All his friends called him, "Hoff-Meister."

The next day Freya flew from Darwin back to Cairns, a two-and-a-half-hour flight (or fifty days by kayak), and then on to the Injinoo/Bamaga Airport at the top of Cape York. Waiting by the lone airstrip was Greg Bethune. He greeted Freya cordially, and then turned his attention to the twelve other disembarking passengers who would be spending the next week onboard the *Tropical Paradise.*

It had been nearly a month since they had seen each other, although they had spoken and texted so often that Freya had racked up a grand in cell phone charges. For a day or two they pretended that Freya was just another paying customer. But from the amount of time she was spending in the wheelhouse, it became fairly obvious to all that she was angling for more than the fish.

We on the blog were left in the dark for a few days before Freya went public with her new romance. She posted six photos of her "Halfway Trip Holiday" that left no doubt she and Greg were a couple. This sent more than a few of her regular male bloggers into a tizzy. Some were in denial: "Much deserved rest for a brave woman, but who is that man with you?" Others tried to laugh it off: "All over the world, rugged he-men sea kayakers are weeping with feelings of inadequacy." And some just let their feelings show: "I think my heart just broke in two seeing you with that man . . ."

What struck me, however, was that while Freya looked fit, tan, relaxed, and happy as a clam in a new red dress, Greg, who bears a resemblance to Liam Neeson, appeared as somber as a constipated judge. Was this relationship moving too fast for his liking? Or was he worn out, entertaining his clients by day and Freya by night? Or maybe he just didn't like having his picture taken?

The truth was, things were . . . complicated. Bethune, who had been divorced for years, had a longtime girlfriend. So in addition to any guilt he might feel, he now had to worry about her possibly stumbling upon Freya's blog, where it would be as clear as a giant trevally on the end of a Shimano that her skipper was cavorting with the world's most famous female sea kayaker.

Other than that bit of awkwardness, the reunion was going well—enough so that Freya floated the idea of Greg acting as her support crew for her final leg along the Southern Ocean. At this Greg came clean about his girlfriend in Cairns—but quickly added that he planned to end the relationship as soon as they got back.

Freya was way ahead of him. As far as she was concerned, the morning she set out to cross the Gulf, Greg had "proposed" that they work together, and to work together they would obviously have to be together. When she paddled out of Melbourne back in January, her first priority was to get her record, but her second was to continue her search for the life partner she wanted so badly. Improbably, it seemed she had found him, in a remote, rugged corner of Australia. During the last month she'd had a strong, capable man to call on the phone, to ask for advice, to plan with and fantasize about—and it had buoyed her up across the Gulf and through Arnhem Land.

She was looking for a life change. She felt comfortable being with Greg on the *Tropical Paradise*. The boat reminded her of her ice-cream shops and motor home in one. Greg needed a female hand on board and she liked being the only woman on a boat full of sporting men. "This is what I'm used to," she told me. "The lifestyle appeals to me."

At the end of the week, they returned to Cairns. Freya checked into a hotel and waited for Greg to wrap up his relationship and return so they could spend one last night together before she flew back to Darwin. But A led to B and C turned into Oh No and he didn't make it back that night. Freya was furious. The next day she insisted he settle things *now*, before she left, which apparently he did. When she stepped on the plane all was right between them and with the world, at least as far as Freya was concerned.

After twelve days off, Freya was infused with a genuine desire to get back underway. Although she called her break the "halfway trip vacation," in fact she had 3,693 miles in the bag and 4,872 to go. *Vasdaproblum?* She was still well ahead of Caffyn's pace and the rest had done wonders for her skin. She was excited about the upcoming "beautiful and challenging" leg from Darwin to Broome.

Better yet, Greg had promised to meet her in Broome in a month.

CHAPTER NINE

Dreamtime Country

Generally speaking, a howling wilderness does not howl: it is the imagination of the traveler that does the howling.

—HENRY DAVID THOREAU

DAY 135: MONDAY, JUNE 1

After twelve blissful days of not peeing in her kayak, the Woman in Black returned to Darwin resplendent in her red dress. In a photo she posted, she's standing in front of her boat with three weeks' worth of food laid out on the beach, clasping her paddle with both hands as if it were a pole on a crowded subway. Her eyes are hidden behind her shades, but she looks as pleased as a golden bandicoot (at least, as pleased as I imagine any animal with such a great name would be). "It feels so good to be in love!!!" she wrote below the photo, except that she gave the word "so" fifteen extra o's. "Even a strong woman sometimes needs a strong man's shoulder," she added.

After a trip to the post office and interviews with ABC radio and the *Darwin Sun*, Freya finally headed off with the outgoing tide at noon. West of Cox Peninsula, the coastline falls away. Freya planned to cut across Beagle Gulf to save some miles. If all went well, she would reach Dum In Mirrie Island, 50 miles west, by midnight. She reached open water just as night was falling. With no wind and a half-moon lighting the way, conditions were ideal for crossing Beagle Gulf. There was just one problem. While her cruise on the *Tropical Paradise* had been a tonic to body and soul, it had left her with something of a sleep deficit. She was so tired she kept laying back on the rear deck "for deep, short powernaps."

Napping tends to slow you down, and going slow in an area where the tidal variance is over 30 feet—the greatest in the world except for the Bay of Fundy—is risky business. At 1:00 a.m. she still had 6 miles to go when the tide turned against her. It was as if she was running up the down escalator. To stop paddling now, even for a minute, would be to squander precious mileage. She put all thoughts of sleep out of mind and bore down, creeping ever so slowly forward in her heavily laden boat.

Three hours later, Freya thought she could make out the southeast shore of Dum In Mirrie Island in the beam of her headlamp. It was 4:00 a.m. She was thinking how good it would feel to get horizontal when the sickening crunch of fiberglass on rock brought her to an abrupt stop. The ocean was deserting her. She had two choices: get out and drag her boat to deeper water, wherever that might be at low tide, or sit there until first light like bait in a trap—a crocodile trap, that is. She scanned the surface for inquisitive eyes; seeing none, she hopped in the ocean. Almost immediately a big splash detonated by her side. In the still of the night it was heart-attack loud. She froze—was it a croc? The other, better, option, was a manta ray—a giant reef dweller shaped roughly like the Starship *Enterprise* with a wing span of 15 feet.

But even if it had been a mermaid offering her a cupcake, Freya was thoroughly spooked. She stood on the reef in order to look for a route out of the rock maze in which she found herself. She had to be mindful not to fall on the slick coral; a cut in the tropics can have severe consequences. "Stumbling around in knee-deep water through sharp reefs in pitch darkness with only a moderately strong flashlight handy," she said, with typical understatement, "is NOT a nice feeling."

She managed to walk the boat into deeper water but had only paddled a little closer to the island before grinding to a halt again. She climbed out for the second time and the water around her again erupted. "I was frightened to death!!!" she wrote, strong words from a woman who doesn't do fear.

Again she looked for a way out, but by 5:00 a.m., she'd had enough. "The reward wasn't worth the risk of damaging the boat," she said, "or of having a croc nibble my leg." She found a "flattish" ledge, sat back in the soggy seat, and had a proper nap. Manta ray or croc notwithstanding, a girl needs her sleep.

DAY 136: TUESDAY, JUNE 2

Freya opened her eyes before first light. She was high and dry on the reef, but as the curtain rose on the new day she could see that open water was just 50 yards away. She dragged the boat over a gauntlet of mussel shells, cringing as she left her kayak's gel coat* behind. But it took nearly three hours before she was finally paddling again and by that time she was so weary she kept nodding off in the boat. Unable to find a decent place to land on Dum In Mirrie Island, she pushed on. Late that afternoon at low tide, she saw a lovely sand beach off Jenny Point that was not marked on her map. There were croc slides on the sand, but she was too tired to care—"I needed sleep, deep continuous sleep," she said.

She secured her kayak in the sand, crawled in her tent, and crashed. At 9:00 p.m. she emerged and began hauling her gear up the beach before high tide. She had three large gear bags, four bags of food, and, of course, her boat. As Freya headed up the beach with a bag draped on each shoulder, every able-bodied mosquito west of Crab Claw Island descended on her nude body. She quickly dressed for the next carry.

Once she had gotten her boat up the beach, she noticed the ugly hole in the hull under the front bulkhead. *Bugger that*, she thought. She rinsed the area with fresh water and flipped the boat upside down to allow the sun to dry the wound. On the plus side, she could sleep in—she would not be paddling tomorrow.

It was as steamy as a sauna in her tent when she emerged the next morning. Just outside she discovered two deep, wide croc slides heading to the dunes. Or were they turtle tracks? She couldn't tell. "My night's neighbor came in at some time after high tide," she wrote, "but they have gone fishin' already early this morning. I'm really getting used to their presence!"

For me, this blog entry begged the question: *Should* one get used to a croc's presence? Freya's success so far was due to skill, courage, planning,

---

* Gel coat is lamination painted over the surface of a composite kayak.

prudence, and luck. If, over time, out of fatigue or overconfidence, she began to lower her standards for prudence, she had better hope her luck held out.

But as she paddled off the next day, she was more concerned about her patch job of epoxy putty holding out. It was the first she had ever done by herself, and it held long enough until the following day, when she met a fisherman in Bulgul who happened to be handy with fiberglass.

DAY 139: FRIDAY, JUNE 5

The 1,000 miles of coast that lay before Freya was called the Kimberley, after a British earl who served as secretary of state for the Australian colony. To me, this rather dainty name doesn't evoke the miles-from-nowhere, *never-been-there-mate* feel of a region known for its mangrove swamps, monsoons, crocodiles, deserted beaches, rocky bluffs, and archipelago with more than eight hundred uninhabited islands. There are also a handful of remote towns where the descendants of people who arrived fifty thousand years ago keep track of the past with the names of the cyclones that blow through each year.

I asked Karl Treacher, the paddler from Sydney who had been so sympathetic about my first brush with bluebottles, what Australians call the area and what sort of reputation it has. According to the well-traveled Treacher: "That stretch of coastline is so invisible to all of us it has no name or reference that I know of other than, 'the remote croc-infested northwestern coast.'"

That the Kimberley was secluded and inaccessible didn't faze Freya at all—she was eager to see this famously beautiful stretch of coast—but the limited access to fresh water, the abundance of crocodiles, and the absence of her new man certainly did.

An hour before sunset Freya came to the end of a stretch of sheer cliffs and landed on a steep beach at Cape Dombey. She had planned on pushing farther up the coast to shorten the monster crossing of Joseph Bonaparte Gulf the following day. But she was still tired, and perhaps emotionally she hadn't completely committed to leaving Cape York and Greg behind. The fishing charter anchored off shore didn't help.

She thought of contacting the boat on her VHF radio, but she wasn't really in the mood for company. After setting up camp, she strolled along the beach to the base of the cliffs. In the setting sun the unbroken brick-red stone flamed into riotous color. It was hard to just enjoy the beautiful scene when she kept wishing she could share it with Greg. She stood there as the shadows slid down the wall and into the sea. Then she walked back to her lonely camp.

DAY 140: SATURDAY, JUNE 6

At least when she woke in the morning the fishing charter was gone. "Too much remembering anyway," she wrote.

Gone, too, was her former resolve to cut directly across the 168-mile expanse of the Joseph Bonaparte Gulf. Sure, it was 200 miles shorter than the Gulf of Carpentaria, but spending four days at sea was still a dicey proposition, even if the weather forecast was perfect, and it was not. More importantly, she just didn't feel like it. "Been there, done that" in Freya-speak; "I'm wasted and it's too dangerous" in any other language.

As she prepared to launch, the tide was rushing out. She watched the exposed rock along the reef grow larger—until she realized the rock was a large croc floating just off the beach. She froze mid-blink, tracking his path until he vanished under water. She hustled into her boat and paddled in the opposite direction, her sights set on the Old Mission Station at Port Keats.

Ten hours later she spotted the former Catholic mission along the Daly River. As Freya approached the sprawling Aboriginal community the locals call Wadeye, a gaggle of kids stood on the beach, gesticulating like hyperactive traffic cops. Pointing at her high-tech kayak, a skinny kid with floppy hair and a gap-toothed smile shouted "*lippa lippa*," which means "canoe" in their native tongue of Murrinh-patha. "Hello lady!" he exclaimed again and again.

Inaccessible by road for up to five months during the rainy season, this remote community of twenty-seven hundred is home to people from seven tribes—a melting pot created in the 1930s when missionaries persuaded indigenous groups to live together. The arrival of the missionaries, a mere eighty years ago, was the first meaningful contact these people had had with the outside world since they had arrived in Australia during the last Ice Age. And yet the discovery of a mummified baby mammoth generates more interest around the world than this living, human bridge to the prehistoric past.

But Freya wasn't thinking about any of that. She needed water.

She stepped out of her kayak and sank up to her knees in mud. She scrambled back in, paddled farther up the beach, her juvenile welcoming committee prancing along the beach shouting instructions in broken English. She was just about to land a second time when she nearly ran into a croc as long as her kayak lurking in the murky water.

Is that what the kids were trying to tell her?

She carved a tight turn and pushed farther up the coast to find a croc-free spot to land. Dusk was falling by the time she had set up camp and walked into town, where she soon found an Aboriginal woman who was happy to fill her water bags from her outdoor well. For a luxurious treat, Freya filled a bucket with fresh water and poured it over her head.

"That felt good!" she said of her first shower in four days. The woman, surrounded by more kids than Mother Goose, wore a cross around her neck. She nodded and smiled. Freya handed her one of her promo cards. "Thanks for the water," she said. Shouldering eight pouches—a ten-day supply weighing forty-eight pounds—she trudged back down the dusty red road to her tent.

DAYS 141–142: JUNE 7–8

Having paddled two days south and west along the coast of Joseph Bonaparte Gulf, Freya decided it was finally time to bash directly across. Pelican Island, located 4 miles off the western shore of the Gulf, was 62 miles away—"a reasonable distance for an overnight paddle," she wrote. Reasonable compared to 350 miles, the distance she had paddled across the Gulf of Carpentaria. Having crossed the 32-mile Molokai Channel five times and done a couple of 40-mile open-water jaunts on the Great Lakes—none at night and none alone and certainly none alone at night against the tide—I can testify that once you're out of touch with land, the mellowest mile is still intense.

"What was one night on the water?" she wrote before leaving Wadeye on Sunday morning. "I wouldn't sleep properly like on the big crossing of the Gulf of Carpentaria—just power naps. I should land in the early morning, or lunchtime the latest, I reckon."

She reckoned wrong.

The wind and tide opposed each other like a dysfunctional couple in divorce court. "It was rough!" she said. "Tide against wind; wind against tide. It showed me that the crossing was not a piece of cake."

The sun set around 6:30, and she fought the outgoing tide from 9:00 p.m. to 2:00 a.m. Going directly into the current, she could barely cover the length of a football field without pausing to catch her breath. Whenever she dared stop for a power nap or to call or text Greg—which she did many times that night—she lost precious real estate.

It took her five hours to cover 6 miles—"how funny!" she wrote, of a paddle that could not have been fun. At 4:00 a.m. the tide flipped in her favor. She deployed her sleeping floats, scrunched forward, and fell asleep. Thirty minutes later a wave dropped on her head. "I pulled everything in again," she said, "and kept on paddling into the moonlight."

And, oh yes, during the night her boat was bumped by a shark three times.

Around 6:30 a.m., a brilliant red sun peeked over the horizon to her left, even though on her right the moon still shone full. "Pure nature," she called it. Still the sober fact remained: Pelican Island was 34 miles west. "At least the sea got less rough that afternoon," she said, "and the tide was a bit less strong."

By the time she landed on the pungent island—it was, in fact, home to scores of pelicans—she had been in the boat for 34 hours straight. But having crossed into Western Australia, she could set her watch back ninety minutes and claim she had only been out there for thirty-two.

Day 145: Thursday, June 11

On Lacrosse Island she had two more croc encounters, one as she approached the island and another as she redid the patch on her hull. She believed that once she was in her tent she was safe, that a croc would not attack her unprovoked. "Crocs are stalkers," she told me definitively. "They're not busting through the tent wall and grabbing you in your sleep. They study your movements and if you do the same thing day after day, boom, they'll take you." She did admit on her blog, "I took frequent looks out of my tent where I left a gap to peek out until an hour after sunset when I figured him to be gone for good."

This sent the bloggers into a "Dear Abby" flurry of do's and don'ts. Don't become complacent, do set up a trip line so you'll know if a croc is approaching—among the three thousand or so daily visitors to her website, there were a surprising number of croc experts. Freya, of course, didn't need more advice as much as she needed fewer crocs.

Landing on a beach around Buckle Head, she got out of her boat below a dune that separated her from the mouth of a small river—prime croc habitat. Crawling on all fours, she peeked over the dune: There, just 15 feet away on the far bank, sat the biggest croc she had ever seen. The armor-plated bastard was as wide as a surfboard and *much* longer than her 18-foot kayak. "He was such a monster," she said, "I don't think I'd have tried to get by him with a small outboard motor."

His eyes locked on hers and she felt the hair on the back of her neck stand like a million tiny antennas. She steadied her hand long enough to snap three photos, the last capturing his spectacular entry into the river, before she retreated back to her boat and paddled away without looking over her shoulder.

The bloggers were newly outraged, concerned, or impressed, depending on the blogger. It seemed to me that she was becoming dangerously nonchalant. I looked forward to my morning Skype with Oscar and the opportunity to fulminate on the subject. But I was disappointed. Oscar thought the bloggers, not Freya, were misguided. And why? Because Australian crocodiles were *Mickey Mouse* compared to South African crocodiles. They were like kittens! he raved. South African crocs were twice as long and ten times as dangerous.

Oscar's lovely and sensible wife, Claire, happened to be sitting near him during the call. After twenty years of exposure to his bombast, she still tries, patiently but firmly, to curb his worst excesses. When Oscar told me Freya's chances of being killed by an Aussie croc were "nonexistent," Claire spoke up, "Don't be silly, darling, of course she could be killed."

Oscar: No, no, no, no, no!!!

Claire: Crocs do eat people, you know.

Oscar: They don't eat people. They might bite, but their teeth are Mickey Mouse!

Claire: I've read reports of them killing people.

Oscar: Their jaws don't unlock; there's no peristaltic movement in their throats! A croc has to throw a chicken up in the air to get it down its gullet!

Claire: They bite you and then drown you, darling.

Oscar: They are nowhere near as dangerous as hippos. A croc is nothing! They're lazy stalkers.

Claire: Lazy stalkers? What about the croc that had a fellow up in a tree for a week?

Oscar: Too lazy to move! You've just proved my point!

It was a classic Chalupsky spat, but the conversation did start me thinking. Freya had heard plenty of croc stories before she got to Australia, and when she first entered croc country they were very much on her mind. By now she had gotten used to them—but why was that a bad thing? When she said she "just knew" they wouldn't attack her in her tent, maybe she wasn't being complacent. Maybe she was being . . . right.

DAY 150: TUESDAY, JUNE 16

Four days after leaving Wadeye, Freya was down to four liters of fresh water, enough for two days if she was judicious.* Plan A was to flag down a commercial fishing vessel; Plan B to find the fishing lodge in Faraway Bay that Peter, a skipper she had met in Darwin, had marked on her map with an X.

———

* Freya says she functions fine using a bit more than half a gallon (2.5 liters) of water per day, including washing up at night. "That's much less than most people," she said. By way of comparison, Marcus Demuth, who has paddled around Ireland, Great Britain, and the Falklands, uses twice that and, no, he doesn't pee into his cook pot.

With no fishing vessel in sight, she started working on Plan B, paddling into the fluted bay, looking around every headland for that elusive X. Finally, late in the day she called her friendly fisherman on the satellite phone only to learn that he had marked the wrong bay. The pit stop in question was 10 miles back. Pity, as she missed visiting an exclusive lodge on a rocky hilltop where Nicole Kidman and Hugh Jackman had stayed during the filming of their 2008 blockbuster *Australia*. Not only could Freya have replenished her water bags with sparkling mineral water, she might have been treated to seafood soup, leg of lamb with Cajun dressing, and apricot pie for lunch.

Of course there was no way she was paddling that far in reverse. Instead, she found a spot to camp. At 11:00 p.m., she woke to the sound of an engine drawing near. She couldn't imagine why a boat would be approaching a remote beach at this hour of the night. Switching on her VHS radio she heard, "*KayakFreya, KayakFreya, KayakFreya!*" Apparently, Peter, who felt bad about his error, had called the Coast Guard to see if any of his mates were working near Faraway Bay. Her water woes were over.

Freya relayed the details on her blog as usual and carried on. Her post, however, set off a firestorm. A blogger calling himself Seamongrel wondered aloud why Freya wasn't carrying a desalinator, the implication being that she should be. This prompted a land mongrel named Murd to whine: "Now it seems that Freya is relying on other people in her attempt to paddle around Oz. I'd much rather she did it by herself than having everyone helping her."

A few more local blokes suggested she should catch fish or "smaller crocodiles" rather than accept meals from well-wishers. Gnarlydog reminded the mob that she was racing, not sightseeing: "Looking at her mileage it seems that she does not stop to smell the roses. She has and will mooch off others if she can."

Freya never replied to her bloggers publicly, but Hillary, a loyal regular, stood up on her behalf: "Lighten up, Murd . . . This is the first time she has asked anyone for anything. Freya will persevere. GO FREYA!"

And so it went until Greg Barton of Epic Kayaks provided new fuel for the fire. The custom-built expedition boat she had been promised moons ago was finally finished. Was there anyone in Western Australia who could pick up the boat in Perth and deliver it to Broome in time for Freya's arrival?

The purists again cried foul and round two of the debate was on. A plucky gal named Kerry took on the mostly male contingent, stating, "I wasn't aware there was some sort of Marquis of Queensbury rules engraved in stone for circumnavigations. Is this some kind of male obsession? Like if she doesn't reject all aid and suffer from dehydration her effort doesn't count?"

Welcome to the new, plugged-in world of adventure travel, where the audience gets to participate in the journey, often in real time. When Aussie schoolmates James Castrission and Justin Jones spent sixty-two days battling their way across the Tasman Sea in a custom-designed boat that was as much space capsule as kayak, they carried two free-roaming cameras, a satellite phone, TracPlus tracking beacon, and, of course, an iPod charger. Their journey, which began eight months after Andrew McAuley disappeared 30 miles short of the Kiwi coast, attracted such an enthusiastic, interactive following that when they staggered to Ngamotu Beach in New Plymouth, twenty-five thousand fans greeted them as conquering heroes. Imagine if Ernest Shackleton had had a webcam on his ship the *Endurance* as it was slowly crushed by pack ice in the Waddell Sea—it would have been an international sensation.

Freya was paddling every inch of the way around Australia—wherever she took her kayak out was where she put in again—and she shunned the sail. That's not to say that the good Samaritans she met or sought out along the way didn't help her immensely. Furthermore, her laptop and cell phone provided weather reports, information, and moral support, and she relied on her GPS as if it were a seeing-eye dog. In other words, she was hardcore, but far from a purist. And that was the essence of the argument waged online.

My paddle down the Missouri River included a number of ball-busting, double-carries around hydroelectric dams. If a kindly soul offered me a lift mid-schlep, I gladly accepted. In my mind, I had set out to paddle the length of the Missouri, not carry a boat around man-made obstructions that were interfering with my nature experience. My trip, my rules! On the other hand, legendary long-distance canoeist Verlen Kruger carried his canoe and massive pack over the Rocky Mountains on his epic 28,043-mile cross-country odyssey from 1980 to 1983. He refused assistance because, well, he's Verlen Kruger. When he told me that the portage up and over the Rockies had been 63 miles—an insane distance even if he had been riding an escalator—I said that even Lewis and Clark used horses to cross the Rockies. "I know," he said sheepishly, "It was kind of a macho trip."

To him, any assistance, even from a horse, would have compromised the integrity of the journey. (Did I mention that he was in his late sixties at the time?) In this respect Verlen reminded me of Reinhold Messner, the Austrian alpinist who felt the excessive use of technology cheated the climber "of the opportunity to test the limits of his courage and skill." And that in finding technological solutions to so many of the adventurer's challenges, we have "thoughtlessly killed the ideal of the impossible."

With so many of the big firsts claimed, one way to make an old route your own is to go more low-tech than the original. When Hillary climbed Everest in 1953, he used oxygen, and everyone was still in awe. Messner raised the bar in 1978 by reaching the summit without oxygen. Then in 1996, a young Swede named Goran Kropp cycled nearly 4,000 miles from Stockholm to Kathmandu pulling a trailer with 240 pounds of gear. He shouldered his massive load to Everest base camp. Not only did he shun supplemental oxygen on his way to the summit, he refused to step in the footsteps of the climbers who preceded him. He returned to Kathmandu, dusted off his bike, and pedaled home.*

Freya could have made and used her own Greenland-style skin boat— she had several at home. She could have fished, hunted, and gathered rain water in a gourd. But that was not her aesthetic. Freya loved the outdoors, but she wasn't paddling around Oz to commune with nature. She grew up hunting with her father in northern Germany, but she wasn't there to live off the land. Her goals were clear: to become the first woman to round

---

* Sadly, on September 30, 2002, Goran Kropp died in a climbing accident near Vantage, Washington. He was thirty-five. At the time of his death he and his fiancée, Renata Chlumska, the first Swedish woman to summit Everest, were planning to paddle and bike (pulling their kayaks) around the United States. In 2006 she completed the 11,308-mile journey by herself.

Australia by kayak, to complete the trip faster than the one man who had done it before her, and to maintain her status as the sexiest woman in kayaking. Anything less would be a failure. Anything more—like refusing a meal, bed, water, or help with a boat repair—would be unnecessary.

DAY 153: FRIDAY, JUNE 19

The largest oysters in the world—the Pinctada Maxima—are found only in the waters that stretch from North Australia through Indonesia and the Philippines to the southern tip of Burma. As any aficionado could tell you, these oysters produce the world's largest and most beautiful pearls. Kuri Bay, where Freya found herself on Day 153, was named after Tokuichi Kuribayashi, the man who founded Australia's first cultivated pearl farm there in 1957 and was soon producing the majority of the world's coveted white South Sea pearls.

Freya wasn't big on pearls, but there was something she wanted, and badly, from the pearl farm. After nineteen straight days of paddling, her lower back and derriere were covered with open sores, cuts, and bites. "At night I'd wake up and couldn't stop scratching." From behind it looked as if someone had extinguished a pack of cigarettes on her flesh. I know this because she posted a mug shot of her ravaged bum (on which a pixilated red heart had been strategically placed).

She landed on the floating jetty and hiked up the hill past a row of baobab trees, the oldest living things in Oz. She found Sam Marshall, the manager of the pearl farm, and told him her heart's desire. He replied that anyone mad enough to paddle through the Kimberley was welcome to a shower. "It was like heaven on Earth," she said of her long-awaited scrub.

Though Freya made no mention of it, with 4,342 miles in the books she had officially cracked the halfway mark of her journey. Despite five days in Hervey Bay waiting out Cyclone Hamish and twelve days kicking back with Greg Bethune, at this stage of her Race Around Australia she was forty days ahead of Paul Caffyn. Were this Mount Australia and Freya a climber, she would have reached the summit and been ready to start the descent.

Of course, as any experienced mountaineer knows, the descent is the most dangerous part of the climb.

DAY 154: SATURDAY, JUNE 20

The 4:00 a.m. siren that broke the inky silence of Kuri Bay set the workers scrambling to the mess hall, and Freya with them. It was still dark when she climbed in her boat, paddled past a small croc—*Vasdaproblum?*—and headed west across Freshwater Cove toward High Cliffy Islands, her destination 44 miles to the west. Her topo map told her that these tiny islands were located on the eastern side of the massive Montgomery Reef, but, given the tidal variance of 36 feet, she couldn't tell if there was a suitable spot to camp. The prudent move would be to drop south along the mainland and hug the coast, but cutting across the bay along the eastern side of the reef was much more direct and thus much more appealing. "It was a risk," she said, noting that she would be 12 miles off shore, "but if I couldn't find a place to pull out for the night I didn't really care."

It would have been so much simpler before the last ice age ended and the sea rose, transforming the lumpy landscape into a labyrinth of eight hundred lush, rocky islands. Seen from the seat of a Cessna, the islands look like moldy loaves of bread left out in the sun for half a billion years. This side of the Timor Sea was first charted in 1688 by an industrious British pirate named William Dampier* and has been known as the Buccaneer Archipelago ever since.

The sun was setting when Freya reached the northeast corner of the exposed reef. Had she arrived at high tide, she would have seen a panorama of lagoons, sandstone islets with a central mangrove island, and not much more. But as the tide drops, water rushes off this slick coral shelf like a river over a falls. Picture a nuclear submarine roughly the size of Lichtenstein—112,000 square miles—coming to the surface with a raucous whoosh, and you've got the visual of the changing of the tide at High Cliffy.

The not-so-high cliffs of the High Cliffy islands rise nearly 50 feet above sea level; the largest of these flat-topped islands is as wide as the

---

* Dampier had a literary and scientific bent; the first Brit to map parts of "New Holland," as Australia was then known, he was also the first man to sail around the world three times. He spent more than a decade in the West Indies and in Central America raiding Spanish ships laden with gold, wrote six well-received adventure travel tomes, and caused enough ripples as an explorer, naturalist, and writer that Jonathan Swift (*Gulliver's Travels*), Daniel Defoe (*Robinson Crusoe*), and Samuel Taylor Coleridge (*The Rime of the Ancient Mariner*) used him as a literary muse.

parking lot at my local supermarket. For three thousand years the island-dwelling Jaudibaia people headed out on their mangrove rafts to shop for the stranded turtles, dugongs, and manta rays flopping about in the navigable channel that bisects the reef. The richly fed Jaudibaia evidently grew tall and strong; mariners who passed through at the turn of the century called them "physically superior" and "the giants of the north." In 1929 the BBC made a film about them.

And then they disappeared. Some speculated that they were swept away by a tidal wave, others that they fled a neighboring tribe. Sue O'Connor, an archaeologist at the Australian National University in Canberra who conducted a dig on High Cliffy, had a more prosaic explanation. "They probably went to the Mission on the mainland at Port George," she said by e-mail. "The Missions provided food and protection from pearlers and other Europeans who were looking for cheap labor or for women."

Once at the Mission, they were simply assimilated. What about the rumors of the tsunami or rival tribe? I asked. But Sue was no fun. "It is pretty well documented so I don't think it is any big mystery."

It was obvious to Freya as she stared up at the rocky walls that she would spend this moonless night at sea. "I power-napped, paddled a bit, power-napped again," she said. She never got more than three minutes of uninterrupted sleep, but she was pleased that she wasn't being dragged backwards by the tide. "It was working alright, good enough to survive the night until dawn at 5:30 a.m."

Her spirits lifted when the sun peeked over the horizon. Freya climbed out of her boat onto the edge of the reef, grabbed some food from her back hatch, and headed out with the tide toward Caesar Island, 18 miles west. As she approached the narrow gap between Muir and Kingfisher Island, the tide began sucking out like water down a drain. With each passing minute it appeared as if the rocks were growing larger and larger. *Better hurry up and get through the gap.* She paddled as if a dog were nipping at her heels.

She raced through the islands on a torrent of crystal clear water. "The tide was so strong that it was easy to get washed past the island," she said. She had to pull out all the stops to inch toward the lone beach on the island.

Finally, at 1:00 p.m., thirty-two hours after leaving Kuri Bay, she broke free of the swirling currents, pushed around an outcropping of rocks, and found calm water and a soft sand beach. She offered up a fervent thank you to nature for providing such a remarkably easy landing after so many miles of serious strain. Freya camped in the shade of the island's lone tree and enjoyed a rare afternoon nap.

She returned to civilization at Cape Leveque. Greg flew in to meet her and a few days later Terry Bolland, the Epic dealer in Perth, arrived in Broome with her custom-built boat. A bold expedition paddler who once held the record for most miles paddled in twenty-four hours, Bolland owns his own kayak touring business and knows his way around a boat. The trio outfitted her skiff and after a nine-day break from the rigors of the bush, Greg dropped her off at the Cape.

She was on her own again.

In the cooler water of the west coast, Freya no longer had to be concerned about deadly jellyfish and crocs. The cliffs and sandy beaches were postcard pretty and dolphins flitted under and around her boat. But as she settled back into the daily grind she was uncharacteristically glum. Before she had been alone; now she was lonely. "It feels great to have a new partner," she wrote, "but it's the toughest thing in the world to say good-bye and be on the water again by myself."

Freya is someone who thinks ahead. Having started the second half of this trip, she was already planning the next thing, and the next thing was a life with Greg. "I wouldn't mind being done with the trip [so I could] move on to something else," she said. It was the first time in 167 days that she had expressed any equivocation about finishing. "But I'll keep on paddling; keep on doing my job."

In case she had alarmed any of her loyal followers, she resorted to Australia's most-used expression: "No worries!"

CHAPTER TEN

The Man in the Grey Suit

Falling coconuts kill 150 people worldwide each year, fifteen times the number of fatalities attributable to sharks.
—GEORGE BURGESS, DIRECTOR OF THE UNIVERSITY OF FLORIDA'S INTERNATIONAL SHARK ATTACK FILE

LOCATED HALFWAY BETWEEN BROOME AND PORT HEDLAND, 80-MILE Beach (which used to be called 90-Mile Beach until another 90-Mile Beach down near Melbourne took issue), is a wide, flat stretch of blindingly white sand backed by the dunes of the Great Sandy Desert. When a cyclone decimated the Broome pearling fleet in April 1887, more than one hundred bodies washed up on the beach, but since then not much has happened along this stretch of the Indian Ocean. It's a great spot if you're a fisherman or shell collector, or interested in migratory birds, humpback whales, flatback turtles, bustards, kangaroos, or wallaroos, but if you're a kayaker on a mission hauling one hundred pounds of gear, 80-Mile Beach is a serious pain in the ass.

The tidal variance is a healthy 28 feet, but the beach is so flat that at low tide the ocean recedes at an aggressive trot and vanishes over the horizon. You can pull up to a beach at high tide and crash at sunset, and when you crawl out of your tent in the morning the ocean is gone, goodbye—as in, something is dramatically wrong with this picture. Having done her research, Freya anticipated having to drag her boat to the water and had picked up a set of collapsible wheels in Broome. To minimize the need to trudge down the beach like a traveler with a gigantic rolling suitcase, she aimed to paddle from high tide to high tide. That left her two options: start at noon and paddle until midnight, or start at midnight and finish at noon.

Making camp in the dark is risky business, so Freya chose the second option. At midnight on July 7, Day 171, she crawled out of her tent into a cold, clammy fog. She packed her wet, sandy tent, a job nearly as unpleasant as putting on wet underwear, and by 1:00 a.m. slipped through the break zone and headed west without the aid of the moon. After more than six months of rising with the sun, she felt like an owl working the day shift. Over the next five hours she covered a measly 10 miles, napping frequently along the way.

A half hour after sunrise she was jolted completely awake when something slammed into her left stern. It was like being blindsided by a car in a parking lot, complete with a loud crashing noise. Freya threw down a brace, trying desperately to stay upright. When she felt stable enough she took a quick look behind. The water behind her was undisturbed—no dorsal fin—but she saw what she guessed was a bloody piece of shark flesh on the rear deck.

It made the hair on the back of her neck stand up. She had been bumped many times over the past months by large aquatic creatures. On her blog she had called them "love taps." But this was in another league altogether. Still, she was OK, and her boat seemed to be OK, so she simply carried on. She was bumped twice more that morning, less hard than the first time, but, overtired and spooked as she was, these collisions still scared her. Apparently, Cape Jaubert was a sharky area. When Paul Caffyn passed through, he was jostled by sharks at an alarming rate. "At each bump," he wrote in *The Dreamtime Voyage*, "my bum nearly cleared the cockpit seat."

She paddled as close to the shore as she could. Around noon a breaker caught her and surfed her unexpectedly into shore. Since she was already on dry land, she got out to have a look at the piece of "shark flesh" still clinging to the back deck. It was actually a chunk of fiberglass raised like the flip-top on an aluminum can. There was a hole next to it that you could easily drop a No. 2 pencil through, and next to that was a jagged tooth, embedded firmly in the deck. There were four more holes below the water line. She checked the inside of her back hatch—it was as wet as a fish tank.

Some Aussies call them "white pointers." The paddlers I know refer to them as "the man in the grey suit," or "Noah's", as in Ark, which rhymes with shark. But a bite of that size, with the power to penetrate carbon, Kevlar, fiberglass, and high-density infusion grade foam, had *carcharodon carcharias*—great white—written all over it. She replayed the crashing sound she had heard—now it sounded like teeth breaking through fiberglass. What if she had still been in her old, lightweight boat—but she didn't even want to think about that.

It's probably a good thing that Freya didn't go to the movies as a kid and never saw *Jaws*, the 1975 blockbuster about a man-eating shark that traumatized swimmers much the way Hitchcock's *Psycho* did people showering in cheap motels. But even though great whites rarely strike kayaks and don't typically target humans—the average number of people attacked worldwide each year is sixty-three—there was no getting around the fact that she had been attacked in a kayak, and that it could happen again.

Four days earlier around Cape Villaret, she had been paddling past sunset when she noticed that her rudder had come loose and was dangerously close to dropping into the drink. Mindful of sharks and sea snakes, she had no choice but to jump into the chilly water, a flashlight in her mouth, and jerry-rig a fix to make it to shore. That was scary enough, but this incident shook her to the core. "I'm not easily shocked," she said, "but this was the first time during the trip that I was really down." She even wondered, "Is this worth the risk?"

Her sister Edda wrote: "Bloody hell! Just what mother was worried about!"

Freya repaired the holes that afternoon as best she could. She did not want to set out in the dark in shark-infested waters, so she let high tide come and go and spent the night on shore. When she awoke with the sun in the morning, the ocean was gone—as far as she could see, there was nothing but sand and mud flats. She could sit and wait for the ocean to return, or she could go meet it. So by 8:00 a.m., wheels secured, she turned into a *Kuestenkanuwanderer* ("coastal canoe hiker") and set out across the riffled sand toward the invisible sea. She covered 3.7 miles in about two hours before the wheels sank in the soft sand, making progress impossible. She removed the wheels, sat in her boat, and waited. Twenty minutes later, cement-colored liquid mud rushed her way, like water filling a bathtub. Thousands of fish that had been stranded in shallow pools when the tide went out frantically jumped over and over toward the open sea. Freya wondered if there was a line of sharks out there waiting to meet them, and her.

She hugged the shore all day and returned to the beach two hours after high tide so that she could land. There was plenty of daylight left, so she strapped on her wheels once again and walked another 4 miles, hauling her kayak like a kid delivering a stack of Sunday papers in a red wagon. Only instead of walking through a neighborhood with kids playing ball and parents heading home from work, she was trudging alone along the edge of a desert, down a beach that seemed never to end. She walked until nightfall and was fast asleep before the moon was high in the sky. When she woke in the morning, her red tent stood alone in a vast sea of sand. Once again, the brilliant blue Indian Ocean was long gone.

A week later, Day 181, she reached the rocky red cliffs and mangroves on Cape Keraudren, the end of 80-Mile Beach, which, measured from headland to headland, is not 90 miles, but 140. It was July 17, the half-year anniversary of her trip. That night she built a campfire to celebrate—the first of her trip. As she stared into the flames, she thought about sitting in front of her fireplace with her son Helge. She normally called him every other week, but now she just wanted to hear his voice. Their conversation that night was brief and restrained, like all their conversations had been. She asked questions; he replied. Over the last few months, she had noticed his voice growing deeper each time they spoke. It reminded her how long she had been away and just how far she had gone.

She had never asked Helge if he followed her trip online, but she was pretty sure he didn't. Still, the next day she wrote on her blog, "Missing you, my boy!" If it was just a message in a bottle, so be it.

CHAPTER ELEVEN

Survival Mode

Every stress leaves an indelible scar, and the organism pays for its survival after a stressful situation by becoming a little older.
—DR. HANS SELYE, AUTHOR OF *STRESS WITHOUT DISTRESS*

THE LAST VOYAGE OF THE *ZUYTDORP* STARTED BADLY AND GOT WORSE. The heavily armed, three-masted ship of the Dutch East India Trading Company left the Netherlands on August 1, 1711, with 286 crew and 248,000 newly minted silver coins en route to Jakarta, Indonesia, for what was supposed to be one hell of a shopping spree. But they hit the doldrums in the North Atlantic and ran dangerously low on food. After losing enough men to scurvy and starvation, the captain broke the cardinal rule of never landing in West Africa, where the crew picked up a few tropical diseases along with fresh supplies. Seven months later, the *Zuytdorp* arrived in Cape Town, South Africa, short 112 crew members who had died at sea. The ship added men and one month later headed east with the Roaring Forties* across the Indian Ocean toward the towering cliffs off the west coast of Australia. From there it's a straight shot north to Jakarta. But the *Zuytdorp* never arrived in the land of silk and spices, and for nearly 250 years no one knew why.

---

* Located in the Southern Hemisphere between the latitudes of 40 and 49 degrees, the Roaring Forties is the swath of powerful westerly winds that for nearly three centuries was an aquatic superhighway for trade ships sailing from Europe to the East Indies and Australia. These days it's used by yachtsmen on round-the-world voyages and in competitions.

The Zuytdorp cliffs were formed in one violent stroke between five thousand and ten thousand years ago when the Earth's crust shifted along a fault line and a long stretch of the Australian coast fell into the sea as if cleaved by a dull axe. Rising as high as 820 feet, they stretch for 120 miles from Steep Point in the north to the town of Kalbarri in the south, battered incessantly by powerful swells that have traveled for thousands of uninterrupted miles across the Indian Ocean. A paddler traveling south would face prevailing winds and current conspiring to push him back from whence he came.

Paul Caffyn considered this passage the crux of his trip, which is a tame way of saying that when he paddled to Steep Point and saw "there was not the faintest chance in hell of landing in one piece along the cliffs," he nearly wet his shorts. Back when he was planning the trip, he judged this desolate, rough-as-guts stretch a nearly insurmountable obstacle. The only way he could envision surviving what would likely be thirty continuous hours at sea was with a partner. That way, if fatigue or stability became an issue, the two could raft their kayaks together and form a stable "sleeping platform."

Caffyn began his Australian odyssey with a partner—Thom Turbett—but the two butted heads from the start and Turbett bailed before he reached Sydney. For months the thought of paddling the cliffs solo had gnawed at Caffyn. He had risen to countless challenges over the course of paddling 6,500 miles through turbulent seas, but as his showdown with the Zuytdorp cliffs drew closer he began to doubt that he had the physical and mental stamina to survive. He debated driving south and paddling the cliffs in reverse to take advantage of the prevailing winds. And he contemplated the unthinkable—packing up and heading home.

It was late August when he paddled from Steep Point to False Entrance—the first and last landing spot along the cliffs until Kalbarri 106 miles south. From atop Zuytdorp Point, he stared down at the swells smashing into the cliffs and surging 30 feet up the jagged face. The backwash collided with incoming rollers to form huge haystacks of white water. "In the aftermath of each breaker," he wrote in *The Dreamtime*

Voyage, "yawning voids opened up at the cliff base, spectacular waterfalls, as the white water cascaded down the overhanging walls of limestone. Never before in my life had I seen such an impressive seascape."

The weather forecast for August 28 was ideal. Caffyn committed only to paddling halfway—at that point he would take stock of the conditions and how he was holding up and decide whether to continue or turn back. After twelve hours of paddling, as the sun slipped beneath the horizon and the moon rose above the cliffs, it was decision time. Without a GPS (in 1982 they were available solely for military use), he could only guess how many miles remained; judging by his usual average of 4 mph, he figured he had covered 48 miles. That left 58 miles, and for the next ten hours he would literally be in the dark. This moment was the crux of the crux of his trip. He pulled on a jacket, downed a sandwich, gave himself a pep talk, and pushed doggedly south toward Kalbarri.

He had been careful to keep at least 300 yards off the cliffs, but as night fell that became harder to maintain. At 10:00 p.m., he downed three No-Doz tablets; five hours later, he swallowed three more and still had to slap himself to stay awake. Around then, the moon disappeared and with it his visual horizon. Compensating for the offshore wind, Caffyn had inadvertently paddled perilously close to the cliffs when a wave lifted him skyward like a monkey operating a forklift. He sprinted over the shoulder moments before the steepening wall of water exploded on the rocks. "There was not a shit show in hell of surviving being smashed into the cliffs by a breaker," he wrote. "I almost joined . . . the *Zuytdorp* crew."

At some point during the night, Caffyn passed the site of the wreck. The fate of the *Zuytdorp* had remained a mystery (at least to Europeans) until 1927, when a stockman tracking a dingo along the hardscrabble terrain above the cliffs spotted large pieces of wood on a shelf down below and made his way down the cliff to find a carved female figurehead, silver coins, bottles, and part of a bronze cannon. He kept the find largely to himself until 1954 when he showed some relics he had taken to a drinking buddy, who happened to be a twenty-two-year-old field geologist working in the area for a petroleum company. It had been fifteen years since he had been to the site, but his directions were clear enough that, just a month later, the geologist, P. E. Playford, was standing at the top of the cliffs holding fragments of green bottles and looking down at the bleached white wood of a wreck.

In his book *Carpet of Silver*, Playford writes: "I scrambled down the cliff face to the wave-swept platform below, picking up a Dutch coin and sailor's belt buckle." It was, he said, "one of the most exciting moments of my life." Playford traced the coins, the latest of which was dated 1711, to the long-missing *Zuytdorp*. Once found, the former pride of the Dutch East India fleet became the centerpiece of a new saga of "treasure, arson, looting, claims and counter-claims, bureaucratic mismanagement, courageous diving feats, and indications that some of the castaways lived on to become permanent residents in this harsh land."

Extensive research to discover the reason for the wreck ensued (although it was a bit late to point fingers or file lawsuits). The ship's anchors had not been deployed, leading experts to surmise that on a dark, stormy night in early June, the 108-foot, three-story-high vessel had simply sailed into the rocks at the base of the cliffs. The ship rolled on her side, spilling coins as if it were the world's biggest slot machine. The swell lifted the *Zuytdorp* onto a rock shelf where it wedged against the cliff. How the panicked sailors scrambled 100 feet up the cliff to safety in pitch darkness is a matter of conjecture. The survivors—twenty, or two hundred?—built huge fires hoping to signal a passing ship and stayed by the wreck long enough to realize that deliverance would not be forthcoming. What happened then remains a mystery. No skeletons have been unearthed and no messages found. Coins and other artifacts at water soaks inland suggest they wandered far and wide. There is some evidence that the survivors were absorbed into the Aboriginal tribes in the vicinity, but no one knows for sure.

Twenty-two hours and roughly 88 miles into Caffyn's ordeal, the first blush of light appeared over the horizon. His night of terror might have ended, but the next phase of his trial was beginning, and it included a blasted headwind. Finally, thirty-two hours after launching, he battled his way through the thumping surf outside the Murchison River mouth. Breaking into calm water, he was overcome with emotion. "Yet it was not so much a feeling of accomplishment or achievement, as simply intense relief at having gone beyond that unimaginable edge of darkness for such a long, long time and I was still alive and kicking."

⁓

Freya reached False Entrance on August 16, 2009. There she rendez-voused with Terry Bolland. Two months earlier, when Terry had delivered her new kayak to Broome, he volunteered to act as her support person for this stretch. Bolland had paddled the Zuytdorp cliffs with two mates in 2002. Freya had read his trip report, a thirty-hour journey that featured a dramatic capsize and rescue, but in her mind his experience was not terribly relevant. He had paddled with two other men; they had paddled in the opposite direction with the wind and current pushing them along; and the paddler who capsized had slept not a wink the night before, ren-dering him a somnambulant mess. Of course, she had also read Caffyn's account, and his hair-raising encounter with the cliffs seemed all too rel-evant, at least to me. I asked her if knowing how shattered Caffyn had been by the passage weighed on her mind as she launched that day. "Not at all," she said matter-of-factly. "He is like that, and I am not like that."

For her, the fact that Caffyn had survived the trip, no matter how nar-rowly, was a source of confidence, not doubt. In preparing for this segment, she made two uncharacteristic mistakes. The first was offloading most of her gear to Bolland so that her boat would be lighter and presumably faster. But after eight months' paddling a loaded boat, she found the lighter ver-sion less stable and harder to handle. And while she discovered this on a test run the day before she set out, she stuck to the plan. She didn't even take her paddle floats, her second, nearly disastrous, mistake. Said Bolland, "I knew she could do it by what she had achieved so far, although I knew it would still be a tough section. She may have been a little overconfident by the time she reached the cliffs, as she had sent her paddle floats on. If the sea got really rough she didn't have anything to help her with stability."

Given the favorable winds and moderate swell, Freya headed off on the morning of August 17 with all the anxiety of a straight-A student heading into her final exam. She paddled 3 miles out to sea to the start of the bowed cliff face and turned south. For the first hour, pushed along by a

15-knot northwesterly wind, she covered nearly 5 miles. As the day wore on the wind stiffened to 20 to 25 knots; the swell doubled in size and suddenly whitecaps were everywhere. Still, over the first eleven hours, she traveled a workmanlike 50 miles; at this pace she figured she would arrive in Kalbarri by 8:30 the next morning, far faster than Caffyn or Bolland's party.

At 6:00 p.m., she called Terry and Greg and texted her position to Karel for a local weather report. Balancing in the rough water was far tougher than in her loaded boat; donning her Gore-Tex storm cag required an exhausting amount of concentration. She had stopped for just ten minutes, but those simple tasks left her feeling queasy. By 7:00 p.m. the sun had set and she pulled out two flashlights. With the moon behind the clouds, Freya hoped the stars would produce enough light for her to see the horizon. They did—for a few hours, until the rain clouds rolled in.

For the next two hours she tried to ignore the dreaded nausea building in the pit of her stomach. "I had never paddled in full darkness before," she said. She felt suffocated by the inky night sky tightening around her. She switched on her headlamp and fixed her eyes on the little black arrow on her GPS. The glare off the monitor bored painfully into her eyes.

At 8:00 she puked on her spray skirt and felt marginally better, but knew she would be feeding the fish again soon. Worse, she was dizzy, which made remaining upright increasingly difficult. Her nausea mounted as the night grew darker. All she wanted to do was lie down. At 9:15 p.m., she jammed two salty fingers down her throat. Throwing up brought instant relief. It was the last good moment she would have for a long while.

Fog filled the beam of her headlamp. She was paddling on an empty stomach in a virtual cloud. Fifteen-foot seas, approaching over her right shoulder with a sickening roar, pushed her toward the cliffs. She braced so often her forearms began to cramp. "I was kicking my ass for not taking my paddle floats with me for the stable outrigger setup that I used on my Gulf crossing," she wrote afterwards. "But I wasn't planning on sleeping that night."

There was nothing she could do about it now. "I began to wonder about my rolling skills in such rough conditions in complete darkness. I really didn't want to try."

She tied herself to the boat and for the first time in her paddling career she clicked into what she called "survival mode." Too sick to sit upright, she lay back on the rear deck, with her paddle across her chest ready for a brace. Lowering her center of gravity improved her balance and helped stave off the waves of nausea that wracked her body. She would sit up every few minutes to stretch her back and shake out her hands. Every thirty seconds, a breaking wave announced its arrival with an amplified hiss and she would recline immediately, bracing on her right side as if her life depended on it because, well, it did. "Without throwing myself into the brace from this lying position," she said, "I would have capsized."

Time passed with agonizing slowness. Throughout the night, Freya chanted two words over and over: *Survival mode. Survival mode.*

Five times that night the wind picked up to 40 knots and brought torrential rain, which battered her for as long as thirty minutes at a time. She was further besieged by flying fish that bounced off her body and boat as if she were a duck in a shooting gallery. It may sound comical now; it wasn't then. Finding the faintest of silver linings, she said: "At least I didn't get one in my face."

She had been assisted by an unusual northwesterly wind that pushed her in the right direction. But around 2:00 a.m. the wind switched to the west. Checking her GPS, she realized that she urgently needed to paddle to at least maintain a safe distance from the cliffs. Were it not for her trusty GPS, she said, she would not have known which way to go. "Survival mode, survival mode," she repeated with each deep breath, blocking out all other thoughts.

What instinct makes one person hold on through intolerable stress, where so many others would panic, freeze, or give up? Whatever it is, Freya wasn't the only woman in her family who had it. In all the time that we spoke about her childhood, Freya never mentioned that her mother, born and raised in East Prussia, had been part of the largest mass evacuation in human history. In fact, our entire discussion of what it was like to be German during World War II lasted around two minutes. Never mind that both her parents had lost family and narrowly escaped death themselves during the tumultuous war years, or that nine million Germans died and another twenty million were left homeless just two decades before she was born. Like all Germans born in the 1960s, Freya studied the causes and repercussions of the war and the Holocaust throughout her school years. But she insisted to me that the war had not affected her at all.

Her sister Edda, who said the subject of Germany's culpability was so forced down their throats that it created apathy rather than understanding, had much more to say on the subject. "Mother was born in Wartenburg, East Prussia, in 1925," she told me in her clipped British accent. In 1945, Anne-Marie Sokolowski was away from home at college when the Soviet Army came storming across the border of East Prussia en route to Germany.

East Prussia no longer exists. After World War I, the Treaty of Versailles mandated that the territory between Germany and Russia be split between Poland (West Prussia) and Germany (East Prussia). So Anne-Marie Sokolowski grew up as a German on a small farm in what had been, and would again become, the northeast corner of Poland. Remote and of little strategic importance, Wartenburg remained relatively insulated from the effects of World War II until the Red Army reached the border of East Prussia late in 1944.

On the morning of October 22, Soviet tanks neared a bridge outside the village of Nemmersdorf. They were greeted by heavy artillery and Luftwaffe gunners. The battle lasted just a few hours; the Soviets suffered heavy casualties and retreated. But people living along the eastern border began to slip away to safer locations, despite the martial law explicitly stating that defectors would be shot on the spot.

Finally, in the middle of January, 1.5 million Soviet soldiers crossed the border into East Prussia. Anne-Marie was a twenty-year-old student at a Teacher's College 140 miles southwest of Wartenburg. By the time the Nazi brass finally called for the citizenry to evacuate, the Red Army was rolling and any chance for a safe and orderly evacuation had long since vanished. Over the next four weeks, roughly 2.2 million German nationals fled. Some escaped in unheated rail cars; many more by sea.

Because fuel and vehicles had been confiscated at the beginning of the war and all roads heading west were restricted to military personnel, most people traveled on foot or in horse-drawn wagons piled with whatever they could carry. Nearly all men between the ages of sixteen and sixty were away fighting for Hitler, including both of Anne-Marie's brothers, so the evacuees were largely old men, women, and children.

Anne-Marie joined the sea of refugees fleeing to escape the wrath of the Red Army. Working with Edda, who interviewed her non-English-speaking eighty-five-year-old mother for me, I learned that on January 23, 1944, Anne-Marie headed west with her landlady and her children. It was four degrees below zero and snowing as they floundered through fields and frozen marshes alongside a horse-drawn wagon. For hours they would march in silence as if in a waking nightmare. Then a Soviet fighter plane would drop out of the sky, machine-gun fire tearing at the frozen earth, and adrenaline jolted them out of their stupor. They scrambled for cover under the wagon, the two women shielding the children with their bodies.

Three hundred thousand East Prussians died during the evacuation. Illness and exposure hit the children first and hardest. Anguished mothers, walking like zombies, carried their dead babies rather than abandon them by the side of the road. Houses were looted by soldiers on both sides, then torched; women old and young were raped; unarmed civilians were dragged out into the street, shot in the back, and then callously run over by tanks. Twenty-seven million Russians had died during the war. And the Soviets, who had suffered atrocities at the hands of the Nazis on their home soil, were intent on revenge.

After two weeks on the march, a distance of 162 miles, Anne-Marie crossed into Germany and made her way to Templin, a town 40 miles north of Berlin where Hermann Göring had his opulent country home. There in Templin she managed to contact her brother on the front through the army post. He informed her that their father had stayed behind to tend to the animals on the family farm, but that their mother and sister had made it to Wismar, a port town in northern Germany. Anne-Marie went there by train to collect them. They still felt far too close to the front, and at great risk they made their way to Lubeck, the largest German port on the Baltic. It was there that Anne-Marie heard the radio reports that Hitler had blown his brains out in a bunker in Berlin the day after his wedding. Just a week later the war officially ended. But there was no feeling of jubilation for the young woman who had lost so much so quickly. One of Anne-Marie's two brothers failed to return from the front. Her father had been shot dead by a Soviet soldier. They had little money, few possessions, no home—at least not one they could ever return to. Their best option was an uncle in Hamburg who offered temporary shelter, but there was no functioning public transportation and it was too dangerous to walk. Anne-Marie's sister Edith figured out a way to get there, befriending a German soldier who "borrowed" a car and drove them.

Hamburg made Lubeck, neglected and burnt-out as it was, look like the city of Oz. It had been the industrial hub of Germany's war effort and thus one of the Allies' prime targets. Anne-Marie's new home was a devastated landscape of jagged shells of buildings and once-grand avenues cratered by bombs and littered with gnarled, blackened vehicles. The family of three women lived in a series of tiny rooms around the city. In the lean years after the war, Anne-Marie managed to find occasional work as a substitute teacher, but it was Edith's job at a department store that kept them afloat. Just barely.*

Freya had told Terry Bolland that she would call at 6:00 a.m. to report on her progress, but paddling again into a stiff headwind in big seas, she didn't feel up to the task. Then the first rays of light crept over the horizon. Suddenly energized, she fired off a text message with two words: "I'm OK." Forty miles remained and the wind was dead set on her bow, but when the cliffs materialized out of the grainy light it was as if she had been reborn. "I didn't feel much tiredness now," she said, grateful to be able to click into a paddling rhythm after so many hours of just hanging on.

---

* When Freya read this section of the book, she was furious, calling it a "waste of space" and "embarrassing." "It simply doesn't belong in my book," she insisted. To state the obvious, we disagreed. And still do.

Just as she allowed herself to think that the worst was over, a hump-back whale as large as a city bus surfaced just a few feet in front of her like a giant roadblock. Scared shitless, she shouted, "*Rutsch mir doch, den Buckel runter,*" which, literally translated, means "slide down my hump-back" but, figuratively speaking, means "leave me alone." As suddenly as it had appeared, the whale was gone. Had it even known she was there? Freya had been one strong stroke away from surfing down its back, with unimaginable consequences.

By noon, 15 miles remained—an easy half-day paddle for Freya—but after twenty-nine turbulent hours she was so dehydrated and sleepy that she kept nodding off. The swell was easily 12 feet, and as she came toward shore the waves were steepening. She couldn't afford to capsize here. Taking a melody from the opera *Carmen* and adding the first words that popped into her head, she began singing like a half-mad opera star. Was it coincidence that just then a thirty-six-ton humpback surfaced off to starboard and began doing a series of back flips? Each time the leaping beast hit the water it sounded like a cannon blast.

At 3:30 that afternoon—32.5 hours after she launched—she eyed the 10- to 15-foot breaking waves outside the mouth of the Murchison River. Caffyn describes the dog-leg left you have to make to get through this tricky section of breaking waves, but as she slipped past the bombies deto-nating around her, a fellow on a surf ski out for his daily training session was only too happy to guide her through. Following her escort, she caught a wave through the crumbling white water into the mellow mouth of the river. There before her stood a small crowd who had heard from Terry that she was about to become the second person to solo the Zuytdorp Cliffs. After so many solitary landings, and after this night of hell, she thought she had never seen a more welcome sight. Smiling broadly, the depleted kayaking diva took a deep breath and did a perfect roll for the crowd.

She is like that. Paul Caffyn is not like that. Maybe no one is.

She woke early the next morning feeling ravenous but surprisingly spry. For breakfast she downed a cheese and mushroom omelet and a pile of crepes and finished with a caramel milkshake. She had her hair done and enjoyed an acupressure massage and a soak in a flotation tank. At dinner she knocked back the kangaroo fettuccine and was sleeping hard again soon after sunset.

But the Zuytdorp Cliffs had taken their toll. She woke up "feeling sick in my bones," she wrote, "from the tip of my hair to the tip of my toes." For five days she was completely incapacitated. "I thought you can't be so sick," she wrote, when she was finally able to write.

And then she continued south toward Lucky Bay.

Chapter Twelve

Head Down, Teeth Clenched

People who are unable to motivate themselves must be content with mediocrity, no matter how impressive their other talents.
—ANDREW CARNEGIE

FREYA WAS EIGHT MONTHS INTO HER JOURNEY. AFTER SURVIVING THE Zuytdorp Cliffs, perhaps her closest brush with death and certainly her hardest challenge, it appeared that the next 322 miles, from Kalbarri to Perth—the end of Stage 11 on her schedule—would be an uneventful cruise. She figured the going would start to get rough again after she dropped another 200 miles south and had to face Cape Leeuwin, the notoriously rough spot where the Indian and Southern Oceans collide, but, in the meantime, no worries, right?

Wrong. After nearly 6,000 miles of paddling, Freya was struggling with two of Australia's most potent defenses against circumnavigation— its sheer size and its maddening headwinds.

It started her first day out of Kalbarri. Just past the cliffs at Bluff Point, Freya turned into a 25-knot headwind. "Head down, teeth clenched," she strained forward, punching over and slapping down the back of 10-foot, whitecapped waves that assaulted her like bathtubs falling off an assembly line. She thought of heading to shore, but the crashing surf on the reef looked impenetrable. "I simply didn't dare to go in," she said. As if to underscore the danger, she passed a humpback stranded on the reef, its death all but certain.

After nine and a half hours, she rode the back of a wave through a narrow gap in the reef outside of Lucky Bay. When she woke in the morning, the wind had picked up and the pass was closing out, so she resigned herself to a day ashore with no Internet connection. It wasn't a pleasant spot. Sand as fine as flour caked the wet clothes she had hung to dry, penetrated her tent, and found its way inside her sleeping bag. With nothing to do, she took a walk down the beach to kill time, picking her way around garbage that had apparently spilled from the dilapidated trailers along the dunes. Then the sky darkened and rain fell in sheets. She stripped off her clothes in the downpour for a freshwater rinse, but it felt more like a sandblasting than a shower. Even nudity was losing its appeal. "Trust me," she wrote, "being naked in such a wind even for five minutes is not much fun!"

And so to bed. The wind shook her sturdy dome tent "to the roots." She took out her one book, *The Dreamtime Voyage*, which she had nearly memorized. She was so bored her head hurt.

The following morning she wriggled into cold, clammy clothes that felt wetter than when she had hung them up to dry and cautiously made her way toward the surf rumbling just beyond the reef. She scanned the water for a gap through the reef, but all she saw was a long line of fat, scary breakers. Still, she didn't think she could endure a second day ashore. Bracing in the foamy water surging over the reef, she waited for a lull and charged out to sea into 12- to 15-foot rollers dead set on her bow. She had her sights set on Geraldton, 35 miles south. Fighting into the wind, she moved as slow as a manatee and was chilled to the core. By mid-afternoon the wind backed off and the sea sat down, but her energy reserves and motivation were dwindling. After six hours and just 12 miles, she saw a gap in the reef outside Coronation Bay and headed in. "I simply had enough," she said of a day she called "an ugly slog."

Having done more than a few long solo slogs, I recognized the tell-tale signs of exhaustion: irritability, self-pity, boredom. Mind you, Freya wasn't complaining, but her responses to the inevitable bumps in the road betrayed her state of mind. There was the woman walking her dog on the beach who passed her by with barely a nod, even though she had just surfed a 10-foot wave onto the beach like a bobsledder finishing a run. There was the grumpy old man who refused her a shower at a yacht club even though she was shivering. The birds squawking in the night seemed louder and the stench of a rotting whale carcass on the beach more irksome. She was indignant about the boozy fishermen zipping along the beach in their 4x4s, and disgusted with the wind "sandblasting my kayak, tent and me!"

I was reminded of the time I pulled into a small town in Nebraska on a cross-country bicycle trip. Since crossing the Rockies I had strung together seventeen 100-mile days. I was rolling east on a personal crusade of the utmost importance. So when a checkout lady told me I couldn't use the restroom, I felt a cold rage that only made me and my self-righteously full bladder that much more full and self-righteous. "Please," I said.

"No," she replied with a finality that ratcheted up my anger.

"Fine," I spat out. "Then I'll just piss on the front of your store."

In fact I rode out of town before letting loose by the side of the empty two-lane highway, but the fact that those words actually escaped my lips was a testament to how overwrought, overtired, and impatient I had become. Forward progress was my *raison d'être* and I expected the world to show a little more support and understanding.

As for Freya, there was something else interfering with her focus as she headed south—anticipation. A week before she reached Perth, she made the momentous announcement that her solo trip soon would be solo no more. Her "partner" Greg Bethune was going to meet up with her around Cape Leeuwin and follow her in a camper van for 2,000 miles along the Southern Ocean and on into Melbourne. That was the good news—the bad news was he wouldn't arrive for another month. "Only four more weeks of being alone," she wrote wistfully.

Leaving Wedge Island Beach, 78 miles north of Perth, she headed off the beach through the biggest seas she had seen since the Zuytdorp Cliffs. Just half a mile later, she took stock of the unbroken line of surf crashing on the reef and wondered if she would be able to land again. She paused in the heaving swell—it was a good two-to-three stories high—stepped on her right rudder pedal and headed back the way she came. In 233 days and more than 6,000 miles, it was the first time she had paddled with Australia on her right. As she approached the beach, at least six separate lines of breaking surf stood between her and a safe landing. Waiting outside the break zone, she secured her equipment on deck, zipped the hood on her storm cag, and "prepared to get thrashed!"

She made her way through the first three lines of surf before a wave spun her sideways. Bracing into the face, she sped toward the beach like a skier sliding down a steep icy slope. She capsized, rolled, and capsized again before she found herself high and dry up the beach. "I could have broken my paddle or my neck," she wrote.

A prudent person would have called it a day, but after she blew the salt water out of her nose Freya noticed that the water flattened out somewhat between the break zone and the soft sand. What if, instead of getting out over the reef and into the deep sea, she were to paddle along the shore? Tossing her hat into what she called a "dangerous trashy game," she dragged her boat to the water, waited for a wave to pick her up, and headed south, paddling parallel to the surf. Her goal was Lancelin, a small fishing town 15 miles south, where, she hoped and assumed, she would at least find an Internet connection.

In theory, it was a viable idea; in practice, it was a recipe for a beating.

The water in this shallow, "flattish gap" was far from flat. Waves rebounding from the shore colliding with incoming breakers were haystacking up into standing waves, a condition the French call *clapotis*—"lapping of water"—and paddlers from Brooklyn call a bone yard, but by any name it's a nightmarish mish-mash of water moving everywhere at once. Freya tried to dodge these erratic walls of water but often found herself "bounced and abused" like a ping-pong ball ricocheting around a lottery machine. Grimacing as her boat flexed beneath her, she called it "the worst water you can paddle in."

Every fifteen or twenty minutes, it seemed, she was tossed up on the beach like a piece of driftwood and had to re-launch. Six times she was turned upside down. On the long stretches where the flattish gap disappeared entirely and the surf hammered directly onto the beach, she simply got out and dragged her boat. But even that proved hazardous as she had her head down when a wave knocked her off her feet and ripped the boat from her hands. She was swept up the beach like a rag doll. If her boat hadn't gotten stuck on the steep sandbank, she would have had a long walk into town—and arrived there without a change of clothes or a credit card.

Still she persisted. "You must be a masochist to get in there again and again and again," she wrote. Relaxing for a moment in the relatively protected water behind Magic Reef, she was, yet again, washed up the beach, surprising two fishermen. They told her that just ahead a 40-foot humpback hung up on the reef was being attacked by sharks. The sun was shining; they had sandwiches and suds and said they would be only too happy to throw the boat on the roof of their vehicle and give her a lift to Lancelin. Freya, of course, declined. "That would be cheating," she said, and doggedly headed back to the sea.

Five miles outside Lancelin, she paddled past five shirtless men straining behind a vehicle stuck in the soft sand. Momentarily distracted, she was dragged up the beach by another wave. She heard the whining engine before she saw the very same car, spitting out sand like a race car burning rubber out of the pits, bearing down on her. The driver swerved in time to avoid her, but in a day of close calls this was the one most likely to have done her serious harm. Imagine paddling so far, surviving crocs, sharks, and killer seas, only to get run over by a car on a deserted beach.

It was 6:00 p.m., nearly dark, when she saw the first houses on the outskirts of Lancelin. It had taken her over fifteen hours to cover 15 miles. She was wrung out, battered, and sore, but she had made it. She walked to the pub and found a fisherman standing on the jetty next to a cold water tap. She had so much salt on her body her skin felt like it was coated in papier-mâché. She instructed the fisherman to turn around and, kneeling half-naked next to the knee-high spout, doused herself in handfuls of water. The stiff breeze and cold water set her teeth chattering, but she didn't care. She had capsized seven times, washed up the beach at least twenty, paddled past sharks in a feeding frenzy, and narrowly avoided becoming roadkill. But she had won—or at least, she had refused to be stopped when she wanted to go. "I think anyone less stubborn or stupid would have called it a day after turning back," she wrote.

Two days later, as she approached Perth, a local who had been following Freya's blog for months paddled out to keep her company for a while.

Soon after he departed, a helicopter from Channel 10 News descended out of the clouds and trailed her for twenty minutes. Moments after the chopper peeled off, Terry Bolland appeared in his kayak. And by the time she paddled into Perth's Hillary Harbor, she had picked up a jolly band of maybe two dozen kayakers, following along behind. Perth is a city of 1.6 million—Bill Bryson calls Australia's capital "far and away the most remote big city on earth"—and to someone who had been sleeping on deserted beaches and eating salt spray for the past two weeks, this reception felt worthy of a Hollywood star.

❧

Freya enjoyed a three-day break in Perth at Terry Bolland's house. But the day she left a "bloody head wind" once again reduced progress to a crawl. She averaged a "stupid" 2.1 mph and landed after a "ridiculous" 10 miles in five hours. "A man on the beach walking his dog was faster than I was [going] that day," she said, "really embarrassing and annoying." On paper, the 130-mile stretch from Perth to Cape Leeuwin and the start of the Southern Ocean should have been smooth sailing. In fact, it was more like hand-to-hand combat. The day after she passed Point Peron, a yacht was smashed to pieces there and the skipper rescued by helicopter in 40-knot winds.

As she headed toward Hamelin Bay, a notorious graveyard for ships 18 miles north of Cape Leeuwin, the Indian Ocean gave her a last glimpse of its power. Around midday, the sky darkened, a northwest wind whipped the sea white, and buckets of rain water made it impossible to see the approaching swells over her right shoulder. "I couldn't see the breakers," she said, "so I had to feel and hear them." The wind was so strong she tucked forward so as not to be blown over. She wasn't tippy, nor was she seasick, but she was keenly aware that if she got into trouble there wouldn't be any help anytime soon.

"Hang in there, Freya," she repeated, as the sky turned black as ink, "hang in there . . . it can't last forever."

When the worst of the rain subsided, she could at least see the swells overtaking her, rising and falling like a giant caterpillar on the move and passing with a thunderous whoosh. "Hang in there Freya, hang in there, it's almost over," she repeated.

But as the day wore on, the swells only seemed larger, faster, more powerful. Or, she wondered, was she just becoming weaker? She answered her own question: "No way, not me! I was full of energy and feeling not too bad." She switched to a new mantra—"Full concentration and power. Full concentration and power. . . ."

Suddenly, the 40-foot faces that Oscar had described in Hawaii appeared for real. "Just massive walls of water piling up on my side, with an occasional freak wave which nearly made my jaw drop." Holding her breath as it approached, she wasn't sure what would happen next. "Was it breaking? Not breaking? Breaking before me? Behind me? Besides me?" Sometimes she waited and watched; sometimes "I had to spring to get ahead of the roaring foamy water." Sometimes she got smashed on the broadside "but I always leaned solidly into them and stayed upright."

Ten hours and 40 miles later, she reached the safety of Hamelin Bay. "I almost capsized close to the beach—how ridiculous!—but eventually I was standing high and dry on the beach, thanking the water and weather gods that they got me safely through that exciting day."

Given the wind—southwesterly winds of 30 to 40 knots, gusting to 50 in the afternoon—she stood on the sidelines the next two days. A local blogger named Craig Fisher who had competed in eleven National Surf Lifesaving Championships said the swell at Cape Leeuwin was in excess of 32 feet. "It's blowing the milk out of my coffee at the moment," he said, adding the obvious, "not a good time to be out on the water." A blogger calling himself Fat Paddler said: "The Southern Ocean is a bitter, mean old bugger." He warned Freya that going forward she would have to sit out and cherry-pick the good weather days because, "The Great Australian Bight has a lot of cliffs that make landing difficult. This will likely be the toughest part of the trip."

Freya didn't seem to mind. She was thirty days ahead of Caffyn. She could afford to be choosy. Besides, in just a few days Greg would be with her. From here on in, waiting out bad weather would be easy and fun. Like being on vacation.

At least, that was the idea.

CHAPTER THIRTEEN

Love along the Bight

Offspring of the westerly gales, the great unceasing westerly swell of the Southern Ocean rolls almost unchecked around this end of the world in the Roaring Forties and the stormy Fifties. The highest, broadest and longest swells in the world, they race on their encircling course until they reach their birthplace again, and so, reinforcing themselves, sweep forward in fierce and haughty majesty.
—CAPTAIN FRANK WORSLEY, MEMBER OF THE 1914–1916
SHACKLETON EXPEDITION

ON MONDAY, SEPTEMBER 21, CAPE LEEUWIN SAT ON FULL BOIL. SURVEYING the scene from atop the peninsula, Freya braced against the wind and watched the spray fan off the top of one 30-footer after another imploding on the rocks. Tuesday brought more of the same. But on Wednesday morning the wind backed off and the swell was a forgiving 8 to 10 feet. Freya launched through the surf at Hamelin Bay and headed south through the pushy swell toward the stark white lighthouse towering at the end of the rocky cape like a giant rook on an empty chessboard. Four hours later, she maneuvered through the standing waves off the point and turned left. After paddling more than 6,000 miles, she was back in the Southern Ocean and heading east.

At noon Freya landed at Flinder's Bay—not to be confused with Flinder, the name of the town where she camped on the very first night of her trip, 249 days earlier. In a journey defined by four big-ass left-hand turns, this last one caused quite a stir among her fans online. Never mind that more than 2,200 miles of volatile ocean stood between her and Melbourne, including two sections of unbroken cliffs extending more than 100 miles and, just before Melbourne, the ominously named Shipwreck Coast. "It's all downhill from here," said one. "You'll have the wind at your back all the way to Melbourne," wrote another. And although Freya likely had a more realistic view of the task ahead of her, she sounded equally sanguine. "I'm on the homerun," she announced in big bold letters. She meant the home stretch, but by any name a two-month paddle through the Roaring Forties stood between her and the finish.

Sandwiched between the bursts of optimism—the kinds of messages that would make it into Freya's "Best of 2009 Guest Book," which she had compiled during her break—were the sober voices of bloggers who had spent time on the Southern Ocean. For example: "In the winter there will be lots of waiting for the right weather, or paddling in silly conditions that you really shouldn't be out in." A fisherman said it was hard to make headway *motoring* into the wind around Windy Harbour, let alone paddling into it. The day before Freya rounded Cape Leeuwin, a blogger in Albany reported that farther east in Torndirrup National Park, the swell at The Gap surged up the notch in the granite wall all the way into the parking lot, 85 feet above sea level.

True to form, a nasty east wind returned, forcing Freya off the water for two more days. The 62 miles from Flinder's Bay to the appropriately named Windy Harbour was remote and exposed, with multiple lines of breaking surf that fortified the coast like a high-voltage fence. With few places to land safely, Freya decided to paddle to Windy Harbour in one fell swoop. Thanks to Terry Bolland, who drove down from Perth to serve as Freya's support crew for several days, she would be able to do so with a nearly empty boat.

For anyone planning to paddle fifteen hours nonstop, the forecast on September 26 wasn't brilliant—a 10- to 15-knot headwind in the morning, diminishing to 5 knots by noon—but Freya deemed it good enough to go. At 1:15 a.m. they drove through Augusta, a sleepy little town—so sleepy, in fact, that dozens of rabbits hopped through the streets as they passed—to a boat ramp, where Freya prepped her kayak as Terry held a flashlight. Other than the clothes on her back, she carried only her GPS,

VHF radio and satellite phone, and a modest lunch. Said Bolland: "It was pitch black and the stars were absolutely stunning. Fifty meters or so from the boat ramp there were waves breaking over the reef. Freya cleared them and . . . was soon gone, engulfed by the black of the moonless night."

Paddling in the dark and into the wind, she covered a meager 10 miles in four hours. An hour after sunrise, she faced a more pressing problem. When nature called during her Gulf of Carpentaria crossing, she deployed her floats, straddled the cockpit with her legs over the side, and let loose onto her removable seat pad, which she rinsed "with no mess at all." Now, however, she was sitting in an empty, far less stable boat, in tight surf pants. There's a rather astonishing blog entry at this point in which the sexiest woman in kayaking describes how she neatly managed the feat without leaving her seat. I won't go into the details (although she did), but I will pass along that she ended with the old German proverb, "In die hohle Hand geschissen"* and a bit of braggadocio, "It is so easy if you are in tune with your body."

Small victories aside, the headwind, which was supposed to back off in the afternoon, stiffened. When her estimated arrival time grew dangerously past dark, Freya called Terry on the satellite phone and told him that she might head to shore. Bolland reported back that the track to the beach was largely inaccessible and persuaded her to carry on. But by 4:00 p.m. her wrists ached and her progress had slowed even more. Forty-five minutes later, she told Terry: "I'm heading in near the Meerup River. Maybe I'll launch again in an hour."

Or maybe not. Even a mile off shore Freya could hear the muffled pounding of the surf on the beach—she had to know that it was highly unlikely she would get out again that day. By the time she reached the back line, each wave sounded like a bomb going off. She worked her way through the lines of breaking surf before a wave lifted her up, turned her sideways, and flung her ashore like a flat stone skipped over a pond. Freya dragged her boat behind a dune to get out of the wind. "I tried to make

---

* While the proverb refers to a beggar receiving an insulting small handout, it literally translates to "he shat into my hollow hand."

myself at home in my boat in cheerful spirits," she wrote, but it couldn't have been easy. The ferocity of the waves together with the seemingly endless, deserted beach reminded her of the wild west coast of New Zealand. She was a better paddler now, but still capable of making mistakes. Although she hadn't planned to stop and assumed that Terry would be able to reach her if she did, not bringing a tent or even a set of dry clothes was just plain dumb. Describing her predicament on her blog, she seemed almost bemused that she had actually wimped out with 18 miles to go: "I was nearly laughing about my situation."

Beneath her hooded Gore-Tex anorak, she wore a fleece paddling shirt and two head scarves. She had mitts for her hands, skin-tight waterproof pants, and socks. Still, she was as wet as a washcloth, and though she quickly fell asleep reclining in her kayak, she woke ten minutes later shivering violently. She called Terry on the VHF radio and was glad to hear that he had found a sketchy track to Warren Beach, west of her position, and was coming to fetch her. Freya left her kayak and trudged through the soft sand until she spied the lights of his 4x4 wobbling over the steep dunes. She took a cold shower while Terry set up her tent. She fell asleep before she could eat the dinner Terry had bought.

In the morning she and Terry walked along the beach to her boat. The surf was raging, but they spied what appeared to be a gulley leading out to sea. Holding the back of her boat in the knee-deep water, Bolland waited for a wave to pass and shoved her out to sea. She punched through the breaker, paused as two head-high waves broke before her, and then sprinted through the bubbly white water past three more lines of surf that rose up like cobras poised to strike.

Five hours later, she was greeted by a committee of seals in the swells bouncing off the cliffs at Point D'Entrecasfeaux. She rounded the bend and landed in Windy Harbour. She had paddled just 18 miles, but Bolland thought she looked tired. Freya headed to her tent to rest and Bolland climbed in his car and drove back to Perth. With Greg due to meet her in three days, "that was the last time Freya would need help from me," he wrote.*

---

* Freya was grateful for Bolland's selfless service but maintained that she "didn't need it."

And a long three days it was, but when Freya finally landed on Day 256 through five lines of violent surf at Peaceful Bay, only a shower stood between her and her man. Greg had booked them a cabin in the nearby town of Walpole, and she was able to hitch a ride there with plenty of time to clean up for the "exciting reunion." Tanned, toned, and thin, she thought her black sleeping-bag liner turned cocktail dress had never looked better on her. With nothing left to do, she sat down to update the blog. She hadn't seen Greg for three months and her anticipation spilled onto the page. "This will change my trip and my spirits," she wrote.

At 8:00 p.m. she walked outside for maybe the fifth time, and there it was—a black camper van carrying a white kayak pulling up to the cabin. Time to shut down the laptop. "The day's report ends here . . ." she wrote.

And so, 6,500 miles into her circumnavigation, Freya's Race Around Australia entered a new supported phase. For those of us following along, it was a bit of a letdown. Rightly or wrongly, any danger she faced seemed less dangerous when you pictured a big strong Australian sea captain somewhere in the background ready to lend a hand. Freya herself had made numerous references on her blog to how much "easier" it had been for Caffyn to round Oz with a support crew. Not only was he able to paddle a lighter boat, but he arrived each day to a hot meal and sympathetic ear. When I reread *The Dreamtime Voyage*, I was struck that Freya hadn't mentioned the dissension among the team that resulted in his paddling partner jumping ship after just a month. It seemed to me that the supported paddler pays a price in autonomy and control for the comfort and company he gains. Freya had taken that deal happily; now we sat back and watched as it unfolded.

There was no lazing in bed the day after Greg arrived. Perhaps she was proving a point, or perhaps she was just being Freya, but as usual she woke early, checked on the forecast—it was favorable—and launched at 6:30 a.m. As she put it on her blog, she was being a "good expedition girl." She paddled far off shore, distracted by "happy thoughts" about her new support crew. "We are both excited to see how this will be going," she wrote. "It will be a new trip style for me and a new task for Greg as well."

Freya's goal for the day was a sheltered beach on the northern end of Torbay Head, 43 miles east. Greg, who had been busy all day procuring supplies to build a sleeping platform in the van, called late in the day to say the track to the beach at Torbay Head was impassable but the dirt road to Shelly Beach, farther east, was fine. Fine for the van, maybe, but not so great for Freya; the surf there was thumping. "Head for the left side," he said, "it's a bit more protected." Freya "trusted her new support crew" and surfed in like a pro with Greg, knee-deep in the surf, pulling her farther up the beach. But, damn, she was tired, and it was raining, and now they had to carry the kayak half a mile back to where Greg had parked the van. Even though the boat was empty, carrying it sucked. Luckily, a friendly bloke with a strong back stepped in. But, lagging behind, Freya couldn't help noting, first to herself and then to her online community, that there was "little difference in landing left or right."

Greg had heated three gallons of water for an outdoor shower. She stripped off and he held the bag of water up so she could luxuriate under a stream of warm water. Sounds romantic, but before long Greg "ran out of muscle power" holding the heavy bag above her head. He told her ("a bit impatiently") to unscrew the nozzle and let some water out to lighten the load, but that "nice flush of hot water" flooded her clothes in the van and that left her with nothing dry to wear save a fleece hoodie. "I was laughing," she said, "but Greg was upset."

And, oh jeez, as they were about to get into the car to drive into Albany, Freya noticed that Greg had forgotten to tie the boat to the roof. Nothing bad happened, but it could have. "Small beginner's mistake in a team growing together," she wrote.

The growing pains were evident again the following morning during Freya's launch from Shelly Beach. It's hard to overstate how dicey it is to bust through lines of breaking surf in a sea kayak. To keep the cockpit from filling with water, you need to get into the boat and secure your spray skirt on land. Then you scoot yourself and the boat forward by putting your hands down in the sand on either side and humping along until you get picked up by the swirly water rushing out to sea. Sitting low, you can't see over the shore break, which makes timing the sets tougher still.

Assuming you get off the beach, you have to bust tail to get up and over the next wave before it breaks on you like a blitzing linebacker. And this particular stretch of coast had four, five, or six lines of breaking surf. Screw up and you'll be upside down, sideways, or backwards and liable to incur serious trauma to your boat, body, or both.

That's if you don't have a support crew. With a partner to provide a hearty shove, you should be able to skip steps one and two and get right to charging the waves. Greg held the back of the boat while Freya climbed in, but somewhere between ready, set, and go a wave swept her sideways, yanking the handle from his hand. That's when he remembered he had neglected to remove his cell phone and digital camera from his pockets. Had she been alone she would have jumped out and started again, but Greg was right there and all she needed was one good push and, *oh shit*, the first wave broke on the front of the boat and drenched her properly and the next one flipped her right over. Dragged face down up the beach, her mouth, nose, and paddling jacket filled with enough sand to pot a cactus. Said Freya: "I saw Greg running away uphill from the force of the water, helpless in taking care of the boat with me inside."

She made it out on her second attempt. "No problem," she wrote, "I was just wet with lots of sand under my hood, spray deck, neck opening and sleeves." Better yet, the 40-mile paddle to Two People's Bay was magnificent. With Mount Gardiner and Mount Manypeaks towering in the distance, she passed seals and penguins lazing on the smooth rocks on the coffin-shaped Coffin Island. Granite boulders as big as dinosaurs, scoured smooth by wind and waves, were stacked like cairns on a path to the land of the giants. She was paddling an empty boat and hadn't brought a change of clothes. The only problem was, she got to their meeting place twenty minutes before Greg and froze her ass off waiting for him to arrive. Still, after traveling alone for so long, it was thrilling to see him pull up. They drove back to Albany so Greg could get some materials he needed to outfit the van. Freya wasn't complaining, but she did mention that she was exhausted and that their long drive (with a stop for take-out pizza) meant she didn't get to go to bed until 10:30. "Too late for me," she said.

But by the end of the first week, it seemed that Team Mobile-Freya had found its sea legs. By Day 261, the sleeping platform in their 1996 four-wheel drive Mitsubishi van was installed and a double foam mattress, duvet, and sheets procured. Thirteen plastic boxes, which Freya eagerly organized, slid below the sleeping platform like trays in a toolbox. With fuel cans, a nine-gallon water storage tank, table and chairs, fishing rods, computers, mobile and satellite phones, DVD player, and a 2,000-watt generator, they could not only check the forecast, but search the Internet for the best way to prepare the snook and skippy they caught. And Freya could wash her hair in water heated on their gas stove and blow it dry before turning in. Greg had an electric toothbrush.

Cruising the Southern Ocean had never been so cushy.

On those nasty headwind days that kept Freya sidelined, she and Greg worked on their laptops in the back of the van. Even with Greg there, days off were for catching up on land-based tasks. "Instead of enjoying the day with a nice walk or drive around to enjoy the scenery, I had to type e-mails, edit pictures, check on Google Earth and maps and charts, and call home."

On the days that she paddled, Greg had plenty to do. "You were thinking weeks ago you may get bored waiting for me all day," she wrote. She listed his duties: shopping, cooking (*lamb fillets with fresh veggies, delicious!*), laundry, retrieving parcels from the post office, and maintaining the car, which took serious strain on the rutted, rocky tracks he navigated each day to the beach.* "But in reality the one-man job of a support crew is more than full time!"

And then there was sex, the "superglue" holding them together—"the best I ever had in my whole life," she said. In the many months before Greg appeared on the scene, Freya snuggled into her sleeping bag with her earplugs at 8:00 p.m. and fell asleep almost instantly. Now the van rocked well past 10:00 p.m. and often again before sunrise. "Greg would

---

* The biggest challenge was finding food and water, as there were precious few places to resupply along the Great Australian Bight.

get the playful thing going again in the morning," Freya told me later. Did she worry about how these late nights would affect her performance on the water? Kind of, but not really. She called it "good stress."

And, paddling with an empty boat with the promise of a hot shower, home-cooked meal and a decidedly un-lonely bed at the end of the day, she started racking up the miles. She banged out 102 miles in two days from Mason Beach to Quagi Beach, and another 158 in four legs from Poison Creek, past Cape Arid National Park and on the western edge of the Australian Bight, the 720-mile-long indentation in the coastline that looks as if it was chomped by a toothy sea serpent. Inside the Bight, she would face two sections of cliffs and some of her toughest days on the trip.

By the time she reached the Baxter Cliffs on Day 279, the two part-ners seemed to have settled into a smooth rhythm. The only dissonant note came from the handful of bloggers griping that since Greg arrived, Freya's updates had become woefully thin on details. A jaded fan named John wrote: "Is it only me that thinks that since she met up with her pal Greg, there's no time for updates? What comes first? Creature comforts or progress reports. Now we know!"

On her "normal" twelve-hour days along the Southern Ocean, Freya showed a remarkable capacity to make headway into nasty headwinds. But for the Baxter Cliffs, 102 miles of sheer limestone with just one sketchy beach to land on, she would need a tailwind. Back in 1982, Paul Caffyn was cruising along the Baxter Cliffs when a ferocious squall appeared like a mugger from a back alley, transforming his placid night into "one of the most desperate situations, if not the worst, I had ever been caught in." Freya arrived at the edge of the cliffs just as a cranky east wind kicked in. With her desperate struggle along the Zuytdorp cliffs fresh in her mind, she had no choice but to wait. The wind blew Saturday, Sunday, and into Monday. On Tuesday it blew harder. By Wednesday the swell bounding along the cliffs was massive. Her lead over Caffyn shrank to twenty days, nineteen days, eighteen days. To Freya it felt a little like watching a stock in which she had invested her life savings start to tank. She used the time to edit pictures and update her blog. Greg, who had signed on to the trip partly for the adventure of exploring the remote southern coast—"something I probably would not have done otherwise," he told me in an e-mail long afterwards—pushed for more, well, exploration.

They drove 40 miles down the sandy, arrow-straight Eyre Highway and turned right along a rough track to have a look at the cliffs from above. Lashed by the Southern Ocean for roughly 65 to 150 million years—or however long ago it was when Australia and Antarctica finally split over their irreconcilable geographical differences—the jagged line of striated limestone vanished in either direction like an impregnable fortress wall. They stopped at the memorial honoring John Baxter.*

Baxter was the loyal mate of Edward Eyre, the biltong-tough Brit who set out on an east-west crossing along the Southern Ocean in 1840. Like virtually every white explorer who ventured across this miserly land in the days before four-wheel-drive vehicles, he came to a bad end. After months of subsisting on snakes, lizards, and the roasted bark of young eucalyptus trees (before falling back on horsemeat), Baxter was shot dead by one of the Aboriginal lads in their four-man party. Eyre was unable to dig a grave for his companion in the rocky ground and left Baxter's body wrapped in blankets and covered with rocks. As the memorial grimly states: "Nearly 40 years later the remains were recovered, minus the head, and sent to the Colonial Secretary's office in Perth. The final resting place of Baxter's body is unknown as all records relating to the disposal of his remains have been lost." Reading a sign like that makes one want to immediately go for ice cream, which is what they did—in Cocklebiddy, a town of eight permanent residents. (Lest you think Cocklebiddy lacks diversity, a sign at the roadhouse states that it is also home to 25 budgies, 1 dog, and 1,234,567 kangaroos.)

Finally, after five scorching days spent swatting flies and watching the sand dunes shift—"it was even too hot to have sex," Freya told me—Karel, her weather man, texted her the report she longed for: Starting at 2:00 a.m.

---

* I have to assume this was Greg's idea, given that Freya has told me she finds the historical notes I have inserted in this narration "frankly, a bit boring."

on Thursday morning, a 15- to 20-knot westerly would blow for twenty-four hours before switching to the east again the following afternoon.

On October 29, Day 285, Freya woke at first light. At 4:30 a.m., she donned her helmet, cinched the hood on her overcag, skirted three lines of booming surf, and headed east. The swell was low so Freya cruised close to the striated, boulder-strewn limestone cliffs that climbed to more than 300 feet above sea level. The water was as blue as a husky's eyes. She was well rested and a 20-knot tailwind carried her as if she were on an escalator. Halfway into her 102-mile passage, she was well ahead of schedule. Twelve more hours, she thought, and I'll be in Twilight Cove by dawn, right in time to give Greg a kiss on his fifty-second birthday.

At 6:30 p.m. the sun set and the moon appeared. A bright night and a tailwind—it doesn't get any better than that for a paddler on the Great Australian Bight. Still, after fourteen hours at sea the first wave of fatigue descended. Following Paul Caffyn's lead, Freya tore open a packet of No-Doz tablets. Even before she took her first swig of water, the bitter pills on her tongue made her puke. No big deal, she thought, vomiting nearly always left her feeling much better. But an hour later, she hurled again.

Freya couldn't control her nausea, but at least she could put a positive spin on it. "Vomiting doesn't make me dizzy or weak, but still it doesn't feel too nice." Dizzy or not, after her second bout of seasickness she was moved to deploy her paddle floats. While the floats prevented her from capsizing, the drag caused her speed to drop from nearly 5 mph to less than 2.5.

During her Gulf crossing, Freya could rest by lying back on the back deck. Here, with an onshore wind and cliffs to her left, she didn't have that option—she had to keep paddling or be dashed on the rocks. When she tried dropping her head down to the deck for ten-second powernaps, she would immediately start to shiver. Paddling warmed her again, but then the seasickness returned. At 2:30 a.m., she fed the fish for the third time, followed by a fourth and a fifth. Searching for a silver lining, she thought: "At least I won't have to bother with number two the next morning, as there's nothing left to digest."

At 4:00 a.m. the first hint of light snapped her out of her piteous lethargy. She removed the floats and pushed on, knowing that the forecast predicted headwinds later in the day. At 5:00 a.m. she still had nearly 29 miles to go. She called Greg, told him she was OK, wished him a happy birthday, and doggedly pushed east.

Then, as welcome as a dinner guest who rings the doorbell three hours early, the dreaded west wind arrived. Freya had been counting on a tailwind well into the afternoon, but by noon it was blowing up her nose at 20 knots. "The towering cliffs to my left felt more and more like prison walls," she said, "but I had no other choice than to keep on plugging! Nobody would get me out here . . . and I didn't want anybody to get me out here either."

By 3:30 p.m., thirty-five hours after setting out, the limestone wall from hell dissolved into Twilight Cove. Freya surfed a small wave to shore and Greg pulled her up the beach. She stripped right there and rinsed off in the ocean. She showered by the van and collapsed into the back clutching a hot water bottle "to heat up and dry out fully." Greg had cooked a celebratory meal but Freya was too drained to eat. With her eyes closing, she said, "I should be spoiling the birthday boy instead of you spoiling me."

"No worries," he replied. But she was already fast asleep. Greg ate his birthday dinner alone.

After a rest day Freya pushed into a snotty wind for a week to reach her next big test, the Bunda Cliffs, the third and last stretch of unbroken cliffs she would face on her trip. "I was not really looking forward to this leg anymore," she said. "The excitement of paddling the cliffs was gone." And who could blame her: Toss the Zuytdorp and Baxter Cliffs together and it had taken her seventy-one hours to cover 208 miles—twenty-four of those in the dark in huge rolling seas, puking, shivering, chanting to stay awake. She had also just paddled 180 miles in five days and would have loved a rest day before tacking on 115 more. But when Karel texted that the conditions would be calm, she readied her boat the night before, woke at 2:30 a.m., and was on the water by 3:00. "It needed to be done," she said, "and I like to get unfriendly things out of the way as soon as possible."

The moon was bright, the sky clear, the sea flat. At 6:00 a.m., first light, the wind reappeared, but an hour later it disappeared again. Cruising east along the chalky band at the base of the cliffs, the rolling sea stretched before her like blown glass. Every hour she took ginger pills to ward off seasickness; every four hours she called Greg on the VHF radio to update him on her progress. Seventeen hours into her paddle, she had covered nearly 56 miles. The sun set behind her and the 300-foot cliffs to her left vanished into the moonless night. She was not quite halfway home.

Around 9:00 p.m., Freya paddled a mile out to sea and set up her paddle-float outrigger. She tried to sleep, sometimes lying back and sometimes crunching forward for a few minutes at a time. Around midnight, a stiff breeze stirred her from her fractured sleep. Soon it stiffened from a 10-knot wind into a 30-knot, hold-on-to-your-hat blow. "Where the hell did that come from?" she thought. Luckily, she had her floats out and, better yet, it blew from behind. Carefully monitoring her GPS to steer clear of the cliffs, she was blown along at 4 mph without paddling a stroke. Her "spooky gift" lasted two hours. By 2:00 a.m. the moon appeared and the wind, which diminished to 10 knots, flipped around to her nose. She felt rested enough to resume paddling and, mercifully, she wasn't seasick. She removed her floats and continued east.

By dawn, she had 28 miles to go. That's a decent haul if you're fresh, but heading into a 10-knot wind after a twenty-seven-hour warm-up is a grim exercise in persistence and pain. "I felt my energy draining quite a bit," she said. To stay awake, she sang "silly old German folk songs" so loudly her voice grew hoarse.

It was 5:00 p.m., Day 296, when she climbed out of her boat. Compared to her previous cliff paddles, she emerged from this one "in relatively good shape." But driving back to the campground, the van bogged down in the soft sand. Greg got out and dug, sweating and swearing. He put a tarp and camp carpet under the wheels, all to no avail.

Greg took his role as support crew seriously. He felt the responsibility of "having to make decisions on behalf of someone else with regard to landing sites through high seas . . . that put them and not myself at possible risk." He also felt responsible for Freya's comfort on shore, and didn't like coming up short. As the tires spun, his frustration mounted. Greg didn't want Freya's help, but she didn't want to sit there any longer than she had to. Over his protests, she leaned into the van and pushed with whatever strength she had left. Finally the tires found purchase and she climbed in. Greg was silent as he steered the lurching van over the sand back to the road. Maybe he was just concentrating. But he remained silent after they gained the pavement, and the tension only mounted as the miles passed. She didn't understand why he got so upset when things didn't go smoothly, and although she set to work to pull him out of his funk—joking, flattering, flirting—she found herself losing some respect for him. But then again, the men in Freya's life always had a hard time living up to her masculine ideal.

Heinrich Wolfgang Hoffmeister VII was a big man with a big personality—handsome, charming, and resourceful. Born in Hamburg in 1929, Freya's father was fourteen when the Allies launched a major offensive on his hometown, a bombing that produced a giant tornado of fire, with hurricane-strength winds sucking in trees, debris, and people. Eight square miles of city center were obliterated. Nearly forty-two thousand civilians died, thirty-seven thousand were wounded, and close to one million fled.

Over a three-year period the Allies bombed Hamburg sixty-nine times. Heinrich was sixteen in April 1945 when the 7th Armored Division of the British Army rolled into the scorched city. If he fought, he never told his children about it, and because he died of a heart attack in 1993 at the age of sixty-three, they may never know for sure. But it is well documented that during the Allies' race toward Hamburg virtually every male who could hold a gun was called into action.

Times remained tough for Heinrich and his family during the British occupation after the war. There was no running water, no electricity, no transport system. Food was scarce. And while most citizens were given ration cards for basics like bread and butter, the Hoffmeisters were denied even this because Heinrich's father had been an early member of the Nazi party. Heinrich and his sister roamed devastated neighborhoods hoping to trade household items for food; when they had nothing left to trade, they stole produce from farmers' fields. A good haul was a few potatoes. (Says Edda: "The family ate the potatoes; the dog ate the peel.") For at least two years the threat of starvation was real.

Still a teenager, Heinrich found a job on a whaling ship and headed to the Arctic for six months. "It was hard work, brutal work," said Edda, describing an old picture of her father sporting a black bushy beard covered in ice. "Blood and slaughter and cold—not for the squeamish."

He worked on the trawler for five seasons to provide for the family. In 1948 Heinrich was home from the high seas when he met Anne-Marie Sokolowski. She was twenty-three, pretty, petite, and reserved. He was a foot taller and three years younger, energetic and ambitious. By 1956 he had earned a PhD in marine biology. On New Year's Day in 1957, he and Anne-Marie were married. They moved to Heikendorf, a small town on the Baltic Sea. Edda was born in 1961; Freya followed three years later.

When Freya was nine years old, she answered a knock at the front door. A short, slight woman in her early thirties stood next to a little girl. Pointing to the girl by her side, she told Freya, "This is your sister!"

Freya did not reply.

"Is your mother home?" the woman asked.

Freya's mother and the unwelcome visitor spoke in hushed tones for just a few minutes. When the visitor left, her mother stared out the back window, fighting back tears. Freya cannot recall what, if anything, her mother told her, other than that she tried to pretend that nothing bad had happened. Keeping up appearances was important to Mrs. Hoffmeister. Says Edda: "My mother came out of a poor background; as my father worked his way up through the ranks, she had a social position to maintain. She cared very much about bettering herself and the rest of the family."

When Mr. Hoffmeister returned home, his wife led him out back where they remained for several hours. A few days later, Heinrich pulled

Freya aside and told her that the girl at the door was his seven-year-old daughter. Her name was Wolfgart—the female equivalent of her father's middle name. She and her mother lived nearby in Kiel, where Heinrich worked. "He told me that it was hard for a handsome man to always be faithful. He said that it was a mistake. That it happened just once. That's all I remember," Freya said.

For a nine-year-old girl who idolized her father, such a revelation had to be shocking. But Freya insists that she wasn't upset. "I was simply too young to have emotions," she told me.

While Edda and her mother each later struck up a relationship with her half-sister, Freya has spoken to her just twice in her life. "I was not interested in her," she said. She paused as that statement hung between us. "I'm simply not interested in people anyway."

If this discovery upset her, Freya shook it off like a dog just after a bath. She was still only too happy to join her father and his trusty dachshund when he visited his hunting camp off in the forest that he so loved. Because he was so often away—earning extra money to support his second family, as it turns out—their time together was precious and much anticipated. Her father was a magnetic, charming man, commanding attention like a movie star. Said Edda, "He was a brilliant storyteller; you'd laugh your head off."

Heinrich also had a sense of his own importance. He could trace his line back to 1650 and had been eager for a little Henry the VIII to carry on the family name.[*] "My father was a hunter who didn't have a son," Freya said.

Edda says that although her father loved her and Freya, if his third daughter had been a boy, he might have been tempted to make his home with this other family. Whether Freya felt that threat hanging over her childhood—what if a son did materialize?—it's impossible to say. She doesn't think so. But it's hard to imagine that any boy could have done more to impress a father—shown more courage, mastered more skills, or stayed more loyal—than Heinrich Hoffmeister's second daughter.

---

[*] Says Edda: "The Eighth skipped a generation, as my lad is called Henry."

On Friday, November 13, Freya celebrated the three hundredth day of her trip with nary a mention on her blog—after all, why is Day 300 any different from Day 301? Along the barren terrain east of the Great Australian Bight, there were dingoes around Dog Fence Beach*, camels near Camel Track Beach and, on Cape Adieu, topless sunbathers (OK, they were seals, not Frenchwomen). But far more noteworthy was the heat. The offshore wind that blew each morning felt as if it emanated from a pizza oven. How hot was it? The zoo in Adelaide had a power blackout, necessitating that the staff cool the animals with water misters, and the town fathers and mothers contemplated cancelling the annual holiday parade, fearing people would keel over standing in the shade. Freya stayed cool enough on the water, but Greg was sweating into his sandals. On November 13 the high temperature was 122 degrees. Then it got hotter, reaching 125 over the next two days. Of course, it was much cooler in the van. With the air conditioner cranked all the way up, it was a mere 93—at least, when he drove; stopped, with the AC running, it was 100. When he dared step outside, hordes of black flies assaulted him.

Right in the middle of the heat wave, Greg had to leave for sixteen days for a previously booked charter back on the *Tropical Paradise*. It's hard not to picture him breathing a sigh of relief as drove off to Adelaide on November 18 to catch a flight up to the much cooler Cape York. Freya informed her readers that Greg would be back and that they planned to rendezvous around Victor Harbor. She described how they ferried all her camping gear and enough food and water to last sixteen days from the van down a steep path to the water, how the packing was "just routine," and how she had paddled off "not without some tears in my eyes." Then she stoutly added, "But I'm used to looking ahead, not back."

And yet for most of her entry she did just that. She wrote about the differences between traveling alone and having a support crew. "In some

---

* There's actually an absurdly long fence built to protect the sheep from the native bush dog; at 3,200 miles, it's billed as the longest man-made structure in the world. And this stretch of southern Australia is the last place left on Earth that has wild camels (up to one hundred thousand). After they helped build the railroad, they were left to go feral.

ways I was looking forward to camping on any beach of my choice without the pressure to get where Greg was able to meet me with the van . . . but the pleasure and advantages of having a loving support crew outweighed the lack of freedom." Rather uncharacteristically, she admitted that given the logistics of finding food and water, it would have been daunting to solo the Great Australian Bight. Which brought her back to what a wonderful support Greg had been.

Certainly the skipper of a fishing charter, used to tending to the needs of a boatload of clients, had the right stuff to support one woman in an 18-foot kayak, but it was the "partner" aspect that meant so much to her. "Thank you for being there for me for all those weeks!" she wrote. And then, perhaps the most revealing line of any she had yet written on her blog, "the toughest thing on a long trip like this is the social isolation." She was talking about the 256 days before Greg arrived on the Southern Ocean, but she could easily have been discussing the social isolation she had been struggling with for longer than she cared to remember. In our first interview in San Juan, Freya said, "I urgently want a partner. I've been alone enough."

So it seemed only too perfect that she hooked up with a handsome captain the night before her eight-day solo across the desolate Gulf of Carpentaria. In the remote crocodile-infested Northern Territory, she stayed connected with daily phone calls. After two short visits, she was sure Greg was the man she had been looking for. His agreeing to join her along the Southern Ocean made the next three months bearable. When he actually drove up in the black van, smiling, waving, and tooting the horn, it was as if her future had arrived.

Freya did her usual thorough job of describing her first day on the water after Greg's departure. She paddled with dolphins off Searcy Bay and sea lions off Cape Radstock and battled offshore winds at Point Labatt. She commented how tough it was paddling a fully loaded boat again, but made sure to remind her readers that she was fine. "I happily put up my tent and was soon adjusted in my old camping on my own routine." She also couldn't help add that she was "missing my partner, too. It felt odd being alone again."

———

What she neglected to mention on her blog was that not long before Greg headed off, he had told her that, while he would honor his commitment to provide support, he didn't see a future for them. They were lying on their bed in the sweltering van, windows rolled up to keep out the flies. She was floored. She cried a little. They talked, but whatever he said didn't make sense to her.

Whenever I asked her about the break-up in the months after the trip ended, she spoke about the ways in which they were incompatible. He wasn't as adventurous as her. He got too upset over small difficulties that she would just laugh about. He acted like a servant instead of an equal partner. He was a sex addict. I was under the impression that she had ended things because he didn't measure up, but when I finally pressed her on who said what when, it came out: "I never saw it coming," she told me. "I still don't know why he broke it off."

Greg is an Australian male, and a fisherman to boot, so when I asked what went wrong from his perspective, I did not expect and did not receive a long psychological analysis. In his words: "One day the gloss went off the whole thing and I was thinking this is not for me. I am a more private person than Freya's out-there-Internet-fame-and-world-speaking-tour personality. Although we got on very well and it was all good right to the end, it was not what I wanted. I feel that Freya was looking for and wanting a manager to handle, among other things, her pending fame from completing the trip."

Reading between the lines, I had the sense that Greg was unwilling to sign up for what he saw as a lifelong supporting role. You would think that Freya would want to understand what went wrong in the relationship to see if it could be mended, or, if not, to learn something for next time. But while it's understandable that her first reaction would be denial—"I didn't want to believe it," she said—she never moved past that. Greg wrote, "Freya's reaction to my telling her was that she 'must finish the trip in style.' She was concerned about her image, or maybe the trip's image."

So although Greg would return, as promised, and accompany her to the finish, it would be as a friend with benefits, not as a life partner. But on the blog and to the media, she continued to portray the two of them as a happy couple.

~~~

The day Greg left, Freya had planned to land in Venus Bay. At first, hot katabatic winds pouring down the cliffs almost stopped her in her tracks, and she struggled to make any headway at all. Then, almost magically, they stopped, and when she reached Venus Bay she actually had a following wind. So she just kept going—no reason not to!—and eventually found the perfect landing spot: a wide, pristine beach with no surf and, thankfully, no people. As she dragged her heavy boat up the sandy beach of Waterloo Bay, she thought about what she would say in her blog entry for the day:

"This is what I like about sea kayaking . . . conditions are changing by the minute, and you almost never know how strong, how rough it may be. Better be prepared and have the skills for anything, or you won't survive the day!"

CHAPTER FOURTEEN

Beyond the Shipwreck Coast

Courage is like love; it must have hope for nourishment.
—NAPOLEON BONAPARTE

The man who says it cannot be done should not disturb the one who is doing it.
—CHINESE PROVERB

FREYA CRAWLED OUT OF HER TENT TO FIND THAT THE SURF IN WATERLOO Bay had risen like a loaf of bread with way too much yeast. For the first time in two months, she faced launching through five lines of big breakers in a heavily loaded boat with no one on hand to give her a friendly shove. The first breaking wave swept her sideways; the next flipped her on her head and set her hurtling back toward the beach. She tried to roll but when her head started banging along the sand she pushed out, surfacing just in time to see her boat fly by her face. The undertow sucked her back out to sea where the next breaker dropped on her head. When she came up for air this time, she saw her boat launched skyward like a breaching whale. She corralled her boat and fought her way back to shore. She tried again and received the same unkind treatment. She tried again, and this time made it.

Ten hours later, she arrived at Point Sir Isaac.

Paddling around Australia, Freya liked to say, was like eating an elephant—you take one bite at a time. With 7,817 miles behind her she had just 748 to go. She was so close she could nearly see her boat hanging next to Caffyn's from the rafters of the Queenscliffe Maritime Museum. But, as she would soon discover, the part of the elephant that remained would be tough to swallow. Ahead lay Coorong Beach, where Paul Caffyn had capsized and nearly drowned. And the last 80 miles of her trip would be the notorious Shipwreck Coast. Of this stretch of *Terra Australis*, where Bass Strait and the Southern Ocean collide, Matthew Flinders wrote: "I have seldom seen a more fearful section of coastline." And he had seen it all.

I thought that being so close to the end with so many hard, hazardous miles still to go might actually increase her stress level. Imagine getting injured or sick and not being able to finish. Imagine getting pinned down by serious weather and losing the race with Caffyn. Of course, I knew Freya wouldn't entertain that kind of negative thinking. All the same, her blog entries grew terser and grimmer by the day.

DAY 308: SATURDAY, NOVEMBER 21

For the last three hours of her fourteen-hour 40.4-mile slog to Point Sir Isaac, she beat into a 20-knot wind. "Not much fun on boring open water with a bloody heavy boat. The only highlight were 20 dolphins escorting me for five minutes."

DAY 309: SUNDAY, NOVEMBER 22

Of her slog into Misery Bay, she wrote: "I should have rather stayed dry than spending 7.5 hrs for a ridiculous 15.5 miles. It really needs a certain amount of stubbornness, stupidity, stamina, strength and skill to paddle into 20- to 25-knot headwinds."

DAY 311: TUESDAY, NOVEMBER 24

The wind was howling out in Avoid Bay, so Freya headed closer to shore toward Cape Carnot. "The only entertainment was to count the 32 windmills appearing one after the other out of the hazy day, again and again, until they were all clearly countable in a row."

She landed through five lines of surf and set up her tent on a quiet corner of Fishery Bay. "I am feeling quite worn out, and am not really able to do much more than paddling, setting camp, cooking, reading e-mails and sleeping. I didn't feel like typing any updates any night so far."

DAY 312: WEDNESDAY, NOVEMBER 25

After a ten-hour, 31-mile day from Williams to Wedge Island, she wrote: "Sorry, not much to say about this day either. No need and no energy to go further. I'm so sick of these headwinds—15–20 knots again. Three fishing boats anchoring in my bay, can't swim naked!"

DAY 315: SATURDAY, NOVEMBER 28

Hosted by a charitable couple on Cable Beach at the tip of Spencer Bay west of Adelaide, Freya spent the day in a cabin on stilts waiting for the wind to subside. "The house was shaking all night and all morning in a violent storm. It felt like a continuous earthquake."

Although she did nothing more strenuous than eat and type in bed— "getting things organized for the last 3–4 weeks"—it was clear that the demands of the Southern Ocean were taking a toll. She wrote "my body was aching everywhere, and I would need more rest than this day."

DAY 318: TUESDAY, DECEMBER 1

Freya hit the water at 6:00 a.m. and soon passed the 8,000-mile mark. She crossed close to the cliffs on Kangaroo Island and started a 28-mile crossing of Backstairs Passage. As Cape Jervis appeared in the distance "the south-easterly headwind funneled stronger and stronger. . . . A full moon was shining and the paddle would have been quite beautiful if it wouldn't be for the continuous headwinds and my general overtiredness."

She landed at 11:00 that night. Despite her exhaustion, or because of it, she lay awake for more than an hour before dropping off. At 2:00 a.m. the rumble of a truck off-loading a motor boat from the nearby ramp woke her from a deep sleep. At 4:00 a.m. more fishermen arrived. *Screw trying to sleep*, she thought. She was well aware that 40 miles stood between her and Victor Harbor, where she was scheduled to give a talk that evening.

She had paddled seventeen hours the day before, fourteen into the wind. Now, after three hours of sleep, she was back on the water at 5:00. "Headwinds, headwinds, headwinds," she wrote, after fourteen more hours of paddling. "I'm tired to death—too much paddling and not enough sleep."

And, oh yes, Greg was due back the next day. But no description of their reunion, exciting or otherwise, ever appeared in her blog.

Day 322: Saturday, December 5

Freya plotted 43.9 miles into her GPS and spent her day counting down the numbers. "I was already seeing the end of the trip successfully done. I'm ready to move on. Yes, the enjoyment should be the journey, not the arrival, but this journey is very long and requires all your mental and physical power to complete as planned."

While Freya may not have had much to say, her fans were anticipating the end of her trip with showers of praise and not a little regret that the compelling drama was drawing to a close.

A woman who attended her talk in Victor Harbor wrote: "I keep thinking about you when I'm doing my everyday things. Your experience has captured me. While I'm doing the dishes or driving to work, you're paddling. . . . It is quite hard to wrap my brain around how big your expedition is."

Another wrote: "You are the Amelia Earhart for us paddlers, but with a happier ending."

Having followed the blog for so long, I was familiar with many of the names: Kerry Parslow, a self-described "middle-aged female sea kayaker," wrote: "I've been 'virtually' paddling with you every day at my office with a huge map on the wall of Australia, a photo of you in the Epic and a flag pin that says, Freya, that I move as you report your location. Some of my office mates stop by to check on your status when they pass on the way to the coffee pot."

Ian Watkins, an Aussie from Esperance in western Oz, was more succinct: "We are both happy and disappointed that you're nearly done. You have been a huge influence on my life!"

Roger Gocking, one of my paddling mates who twice tried to climb Mount Everest, wrote: "Freya, people make a big production out of climbing Mount Everest, but what you have done makes climbing Everest look like a stroll in the park by comparison."

And there was Sandy Robson. Two years earlier, she had begun her own odyssey from Caffyn's Cove; 162 days later, a cheeky crocodile persuaded her to head home. Sandy had been friends with Andrew McAuley, the only other person to solo the Gulf of Carpentaria, and she wrote, "Andrew once said to me that it would be good to see this trip knocked off by a woman! There have been so many attempts. . . . With your good luck, determination and strength you have done it! Your EPIC adventure has all the excitement, thrills, chills, romance and moral fiber of a block-buster movie!"

Still battling harsh conditions, her own fatigue, and perhaps the emotional strain of being with Greg but not *with* him, Freya didn't have the time or desire to respond to this outpouring of goodwill. On December 10, Day 327, she wrote, simply: "My arrival at Caffyn Cove in Queens-cliff, Melbourne, will probably be Tuesday, December 15th, before slack tide around noon."

After posting the dates of her Q&A in Melbourne and subsequent appearance in Sydney, she informed everyone that the camper van was for sale (including the plates, cutlery, pots, pans, portable gas stove, shovel, and a spare fuel canister). And for the Europeans following along at home, she included her arrival time at the Hamburg Airport.

On the 332nd day of her journey, she woke at Point Addis. Just 24 miles remained in a circle 8,565 miles long. At 6:30 a.m. Greg gave her a final shove off the beach. In a fitting twist, on her last day of paddling she cruised by Point Impossible, one of Australia's few official nudist beaches. If she spied any bare bums from her vantage point on the water, she didn't mention it.

When she rounded Point Lonsdale where an elegant white lighthouse towers over the entrance to Port Phillip Bay, a cadre of kayakers sat waiting for her, bobbing on the waves. The pack grew as they approached the beach at Victoria Park. One paddler lit a flare, filling the air with orange smoke. A banner was stretched across the water to serve as a finish line and her escort dropped back so that she could pass under it alone. It read:

CONGRATULATIONS
FREYA HOFFMEISTER
First woman to circumnavigate Australia by Sea Kayak

The tiny cannon fired for the second time in a year. Two members of the Victoria Sea Kayak Club waded out into the water to shower her with champagne. Squinting from the sting of fermented bubbly, Freya did a ceremonious roll for the crowd. Well, not so ceremonious: "I had to get rid of that stinky champagne," she said. Finally, she grounded her boat onto the beach that she had left nearly a year earlier.

But it wasn't quite over yet. She had paddled under the banner without a visible sign of celebration, so a photographer asked if she could back up and do it again with more emotion. This time she hoisted her paddle over her head in victory. When she hit the sand she jumped out and walked purposely up the beach to the modest crowd that had gathered. Cameras clicked; reporters reported. The mayor of Queenscliff read a proclamation. Freya smiled and answered all the questions that came her way, and even did her trademark headstand in her kayak. But when I watched the video of her historic landing, I was struck by how she seemed to endure, rather than enjoy, the champagne, speeches, and applause. She seemed almost irritated by reporters' questions, standard stuff like: "Did you see sharks?" "Were you scared by the crocs?" or "How many miles did you average each day?"

Many months later I asked her to describe how she felt that day—or, more correctly, how she *didn't* feel. She didn't feel jubilant, she didn't feel relieved, she didn't feel triumphant. "I expected to make it all along," she said, "so really it was just another day."

I let her words sink in before I asked a few more questions that only solicited the same kind of answer. I shouldn't have been surprised—her response was perfectly in keeping with everything I knew about her. But rational or not, it rankled that a person who had done something that I wished I had done—but knew deep down I could not have done—had showed less joy at the *fait accompli* than is normally elicited by finding a parking spot in midtown Manhattan. Besides, I had *worried* about her, on her Gulf crossing, camped in croc territory, battling the Zuytdorp Cliffs. If it was all so easy, why were we all so worried?

On my trip down the Missouri River, I was in North Dakota bashing into the wind on Lake Oahe, a 265-mile-long reservoir. The wind died down at night, so I got up earlier each day and paddled until I was blown off the water. One morning I was out by 4:30 a.m., but just two hours later frigid whitecaps broke over the bow, filling the cockpit with water. I headed to shore and dragged my boat up the bank, picturing another long, wasted day stuck in my tent. A wave broke on the beach and the boat slammed into the back of my legs, knocking me into the muck. "Fuck you, Missouri River," I screamed as if confronting an assailant. "Just fucking fuck off!" My rant lasted a good three minutes. While there was no one to hear, I felt unnerved that I had become so unglued. But adventurers far more hardcore than I have admitted to having similar meltdowns when fatigue, fear, and frustration reach a certain level.

But Freya is in a category of her own. Her ability to control her emotions—not just to hide them, but to actually control them—is part of what made her trip possible. She felt fear and loneliness; she felt heartache over her disappointment with Greg. She missed her son. She suffered the kind of tedium that can actually make you mad. But she rarely let her emotions influence her decisions or behavior, or her fundamental attitude toward her trip.

Perception also played a part. The experts saw paddling alone around Australia as an impossibility; Freya saw failing as an impossibility. All she needed to know about the trip is that Paul Caffyn had completed it. He may have been a paddling legend, but she knew the man, and felt she was more than a match for him. After all, he sometimes complained. He sometimes felt sorry for himself.

Given who Freya is, it would be important for her to have us believe that her trip was easy—as in, *Vasdaproblum?* But after spending a year following her trip in real time and another year talking to her about it,

I have, almost reluctantly, come to the conclusion that it actually *was* easy. To try and separate the paddler from the paddle has proven to be a fruitless exercise—they are one and the same. When I first met Freya, I had asked myself what it would be like to paddle without fear. I now had my answer. As a display of grace and guts under pressure, her trip stands alone, a performance that resonates with power and a kind of beauty.

And it didn't hurt that the stubborn sheila did it dressed all in black.

EPILOGUE

WAY BACK IN HAWAII, FREYA ASKED ME IF I WANTED TO WRITE A BOOK about her trip. "You need to do it first," I said, thinking she had a snowball's chance in a sand dune of pulling it off. Once she returned home, she asked again, and then a few more times. I felt conflicted: The accomplishment was beyond amazing, but the person continued to baffle and even frustrate me—particularly her refusal to even feign humility.

But I started reading her blog again and halfway through it hit me like a flounder to the side of the head: This was not only the greatest self-propelled boat trip ever done by a woman, but one of the three or four greatest in the history of sea kayaking.

Normally, a list of the greatest kayak trips includes four ocean crossings. Franz Romer, a German World War I veteran, made the first recorded crossing of the Atlantic by kayak in 1928, spending fifty-eight days at sea. He launched from the Canary Islands, off the coast of Spain, and touched down in the Virgin Islands. From there he planned to island-hop to New York, but was lost at sea after leaving Puerto Rico. In 1956 Dr. Hannes Linndemann crossed from the Canary Islands to the Bahamas in a Klepper sea kayak in seventy-two days, a journey he wrote about in his book *Alone at Sea*. In 1987, Ed Gillet left Monterey, California, with six hundred pounds of food and gear. Sixty-three days and 2,200 miles later, he arrived in Maui starving and half-mad. And in 2001, Peter Bray became the first to paddle the frigid North Atlantic west to east, without the benefit of trade winds.

While each of these trips required bollocks of steel, they don't make my list. The first three adventurers covered countless miles with the aid of a sail, and while Bray paddled, he was in a huge, self-enclosed boat with a sleeping compartment—a craft that resembled a rowing capsule and a tiny sailboat, minus the sail. You will find nothing like it listed under "Kayak" in any boat-maker's catalogue.

When you're looking for a comparable sea kayak trip—in the sea— you have Caffyn's masterpiece and the little-known, seven-year odyssey of

Oskar Speck, a twenty-five-year-old unemployed electrician from Hamburg who left Germany during the Depression in search of a job. Paddling his folding kayak down the Danube River, at some point he decided simply to carry on paddling, past the Middle East, India, and Southeast Asia and on to Cape York. He arrived in Australia in 1939—just in time to be interred as an enemy foreigner. While he had been at sea, Australia and Germany had gone to war.

Freya's trip belonged on this very short list of all-time great sea kayak trips. It didn't fit the mold of the adventure stories I was used to. She did not stagger to the finish, humbled by Mother Nature and just grateful to be alive. She strolled in, a bit tired but perfectly healthy, and didn't bother to raise her arms.

But that's what made her story so hard to walk away from. How was that possible? How was *she* possible?

"I'll write it," I told her, "but you might not like it."

Game on.

Circumnavigations of Australia:
Freya Hoffmeister v. Paul Caffyn

When Paul Caffyn rounded Australia in 1981, his sole objective was to complete the journey without dying. Because Freya couldn't be the first, her objective was to be the fastest. By cutting across the Gulf of Carpentaria, she increased her risk but paddled 855 miles less. Reduced to the bare essentials, their respective trips looked like this:

	Freya Hoffmeister	**Paul Caffyn**
Trip dates	Jan. 18, 2009–Dec. 15, 2009	Dec. 28, 1980–Dec. 23, 1981
Trip days	332	360
Paddling days	245	257
% of trip with support crew	20	100
Total miles paddled	8,565 (13,790 km)	9,420 (16,160 km)
Average miles per day	35.0 (55 km)	36.7 (59 km)
Average hours per day	10.8	Not available
Nights on the water	13	3
Pounds lost	9–11	15
Cost of trip	Says Freya: "No idea at all, and I won't like any number in it."	AUS $10,647.43 "Absolute shoestring budget," he wrote.

Acknowledgments

Mark Twain once said, "Courage is resistance to fear . . . not absence of fear." It's a line I find comforting because I'm easily scared, and not just by the obvious stuff—high mountains, big seas, hostile audiences. I've also been scared by rush-hour traffic, small talk at parties, and major commitments, such as signing a book contract. Given that my lifelong tug of war with fear has consumed an inordinate amount of time, thought, and energy, it's probably not a coincidence that I wound up writing about a woman who wrestled that demon to the ground a long time ago. Thus my first thanks go to Freya, for refusing to take "no" for an answer and for being so spectacularly unsympathetic to any form of procrastination on my part.

Then there's a long list of people who generously provided support, information, and insight and helped make this story more interesting and dramatic than I could have managed alone. My agent, Barbara Moulton, herself a literate jock, hopped enthusiastically onboard the first time I told her about this bold German woman. Barbara read each chapter as it was written, and her perceptive comments helped shape the book. I'm also grateful to the staff at Globe Pequot Press: editor Holly Rubino, assistant editor Greg Hyman, and copy editor Josh Rosenberg, who together tightened the manuscript considerably. (It's also worth noting that Holly, who lives in a refined corner of Connecticut, does a frighteningly good Brooklyn accent.) I'd also like to thank the magazine editors who published my early articles about Freya: Jeff Moag at *Canoe & Kayak*, Charles Coxe at *Men's Journal*, and Rich Parkin at *Ocean Kayak*.

Special thanks to a few key readers who gave me invaluable feedback along the way. My brother Marshall provided some clear-sighted advice early on that likely saved me from a major rewrite later. Rob Mousley, a South African paddler who runs the terrific website Surfski.info, read each chapter aloud to his family and then reported back; I'm embarrassed to say how much I grew to depend on their positive responses. A grateful nod to Andy "Z-Man" Zlotnick, a wise old friend with a refined literary sensibility. Others who gave me helpful feedback are Kenny Howell, kayak guide, surf ski racer, and overall good dude and my young charge, Willa Glickman, the best reader I know.

I benefited greatly from the published work of writers: *Keep Australia on Your Left*, penned by my good friend Eric Stiller; Bill Bryson's painfully funny *A Sunburned Country*; *On the Road* by Tony Horwitz; *Into the Wild* by John Krakauer; *Crossing the Ditch* by James Castrission; *Fatal Shores* by Robert Hughes; *Carpet of Silver* by Phillip Playford; *The Happy Isles of Oceania* by Paul Theroux; *The Devil's Teeth* by Susan Casey; *Songlines* by Bruce Chatwin; *Breath* by Tim Winton; *Kayak across the Atlantic* by Peter Bray; *Tracks* by Robyn Davidson; and, most important, *The Dreamtime Voyage* by Paul Caffyn. A friend to expedition kayakers around the world, Caffyn also answered my many e-mails, for which I'm grateful.

A hearty thanks to Edda Stentiford, Freya's older sister. Analytical, generous, and wise, Edda was enormously helpful in fleshing out the story of our complex heroine. For country-specific insight and analysis, I owe my friends Dorian Wolter and Marcus Demuth, terrific paddlers who conveniently happen to be German. The Australians who provided insider information and kind hospitality during my stay in their country include the urbane, metrosexual Karl Treacher; Dean Gardiner, fish-monger extraordinaire; Jacqui and Tony King from Team Epic; Richard and Annemarie Eadie in Perth; latte-swilling, paddling beasts Jeremy Cotter and Caine Eckstein on the Gold Coast; and my man from Maroochydore, Marty Kenny, who, after many beers one night, taught me how to pronounce the name of his hometown. Others who were good enough to answer questions and provide invaluable background information include Greg Stamer, Greg Bethune, Dave Winkworth, Terry Bolland, David Golightly, Les Bognar, Lawrence Geoghegan, Chris Cunningham, Sue O'Connor, Craig Fisher, Hayden Kenny, Dale Ponsford, Karel Vissel, Sandy Robson, and Justin Curgenven.

And cheers to my ever-helpful, always abusive paddling mentors and mates Oscar Chalupsky and Greg Barton, whose company, Epic Kayaks, was Freya's biggest sponsor. Oscar, in particular, provided copious analysis and endless predictions, at least one of which was correct: He said Freya wouldn't get eaten by a saltwater crocodile, and she didn't.

The only person with whom I discussed Freya more than Oscar was my wife, Beth Umland. Beth provided more than a sounding board; as my chief editor, her perspective and deft writing helped broaden a good adventure yarn into something more nuanced. Without her assistance, this book, whatever its shortcomings, would be much less interesting. Writing it certainly would have been much less fun.

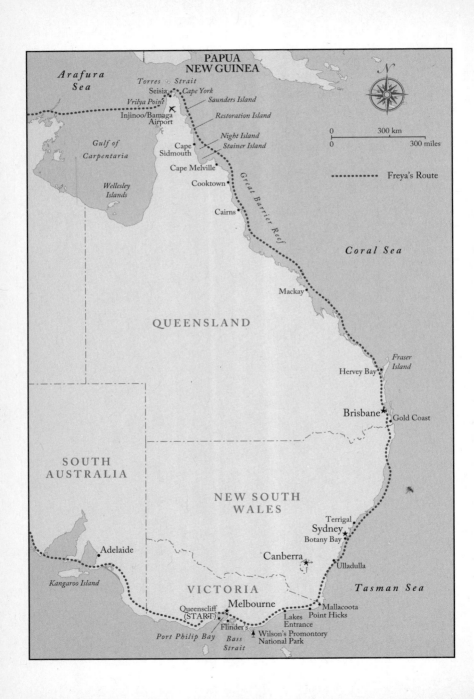

PAPUA NEW GUINEA

Arafura Sea

Torres Strait
Seisia
Cape York
Vrilya Point
Saunders Island
Injinoo/Bamaga Airport
Restoration Island

Gulf of Carpentaria

Cape Sidmouth
Night Island
Stainer Island

Cape Melville

Cooktown

Wellesley Islands

Cairns

Great Barrier Reef

Coral Sea

Mackay

QUEENSLAND

Fraser Island

Hervey Bay

Brisbane
Gold Coast

SOUTH AUSTRALIA

NEW SOUTH WALES

Adelaide

Terrigal
Sydney
Botany Bay

Canberra

Ulladulla

Kangaroo Island

VICTORIA

Tasman Sea

Queenscliff (START)
Melbourne
Mallacoota
Point Hicks
Lakes Entrance

Flinder's
Wilson's Promontory National Park

Port Philip Bay
Bass Strait

300 km
300 miles

•••••• Freya's Route

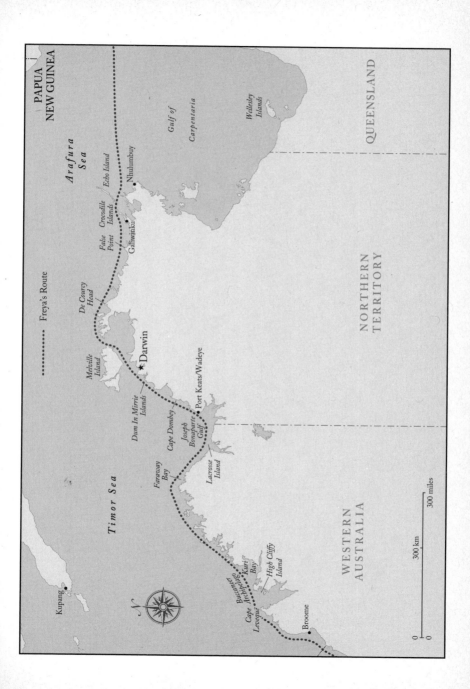

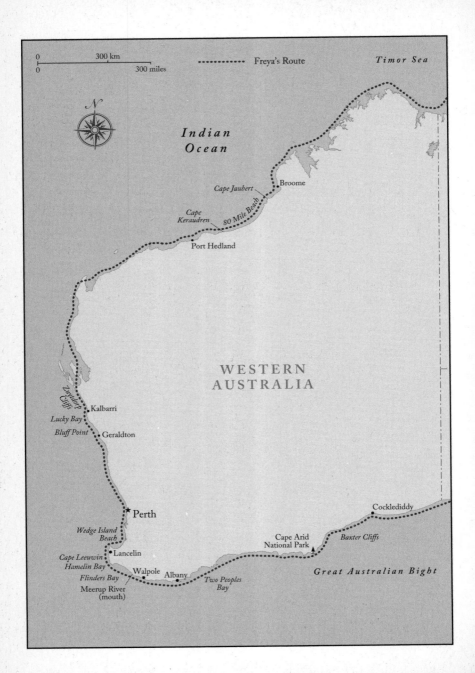

0 ⟞⟞⟞⟞ 300 km
0 ⟞⟞⟞⟞ 300 miles

•••••••• Freya's Route

Timor Sea

*Indian
Ocean*

Cape Jaubert ••• Broome

*Cape
Keraudren*

80 Mile Beach

Port Hedland

**WESTERN
AUSTRALIA**

*Zuytdorp
Cliffs*

• Kalbarri

Lucky Bay
Bluff Point • Geraldton

★ Perth

Cocklediddy

*Wedge Island
Beach*

Cape Arid
National Park

Baxter Cliffs

Cape Leeuwin
Hamelin Bay • Lancelin
Flinders Bay Walpole • Albany
Meerup River
(mouth)

*Two Peoples
Bay*

Great Australian Bight

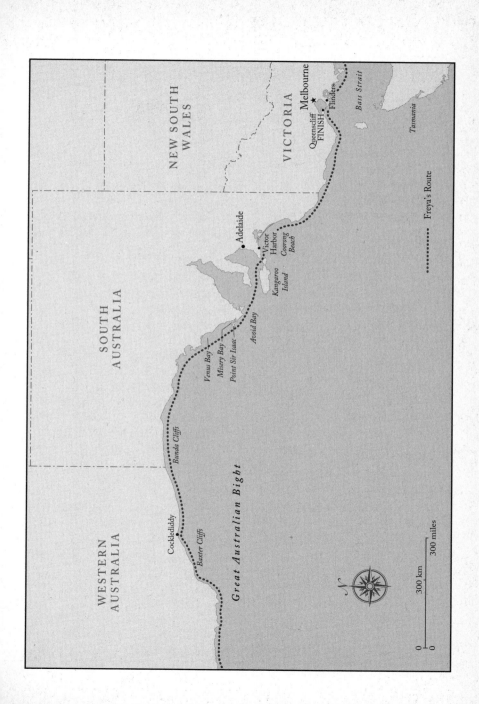

INDEX

About the Author

Joe Glickman is a freelance writer and recipient of the Lowell Thomas award for travel writing. His work has appeared in *Outside, Men's Journal, National Geographic Adventure, Backpacker, Canoe & Kayak, US,* the *Los Angeles Times Sunday Magazine,* the *Washington Post,* and the *New York Times.* He is the author of *To the Top, The Kayak Companion,* and *The Idiot's Guide to Weight Lifting.* A two-time member of the US National Marathon Kayak Team, he lives in Brooklyn, New York, with his wife, daughter, and a few animals.